Sheila Stephen's guiding hand through "The Mystery School of Grief," maps a process for each of us to delve into, interpret, and align with our hearts, initiating a pathway to healing. Her Mystery School "secrets" are filled with deep wisdom stemming from rich and challenging life experiences which instill the reader with faith in her expertise. "The Mystery School of Grief" creates an intense hope for the reader that the sun will shine more brightly tomorrow. This book is a must for anyone who is challenged by a grave loss and is ready to embrace the light within; I highly recommend it.

> *- Candia Sanders*
> *author of "Soul Rays: Discover the Vibratory Frequency of Your Soul"*
> *www.candiasanders.com*

I loved this book. I started underlining everything I liked, and I had to stop - because I was underlining everything! It's full of so much love. And because of Sheila's book, I had my own amazing experiences feeling the power of my brother's loving spirit through Red-Tailed Hawks and Pennies from Heaven.

> *- Frances Newham*

"The Mystery School of Grief" is a tour de force of inspiration for those who are healing from the loss of a loved one. Sheila Stephens lovingly takes the reader through the multiple levels and aspects of grieving with poignant detail and heartfelt tenderness. Her thoughtful, practical suggestions will assist anyone who is seeking a return to Love and Peace.

> *- Judy Black*
> *"Parting the Clouds of Grief; a Mother's Memoir," soon to be released*

Sheila Stephens' new book "The Mystery School of Grief' is an uplifting and inspiring work describing her transformational experiences while grieving the sudden loss of her beloved husband Allen. I had the honor of meeting Allen and Sheila and being touched by their great love for each other. I saw

Allen in the morning on the day of the accident. Usually we would have a quick conversation at the front door while he made sure to keep to his schedule. On this day we called out a greeting across the cul-de-sac, he smiled broadly and waved a big wide arc of a wave. It was the last time I would see this bright and generous man in the body at least.

Sheila's moving and insightful book describes the ways in which Allen would show himself to his beloved as she mourns his loss. In a culture that has found difficult the conversations of death and grieving, this book celebrates a love that continues to grow and serves as a comforting and inspiring companion for anyone encountering the mystery school of Grief.

- Bev Martin
Founder, Navigate Your Calling, www.bevmartin.com

After reading this book, you'll never grieve the same again. Sheila Stephens fills these pages with pearls of wisdom to brighten your life with a love that never ends. My own grief started to soften and heal as I read even the first chapters. It's a refreshing new paradigm for deep and heartfelt healing. Sheila demonstrates that if loss is treated as a pathway to something greater, it changes barriers into doorways. I'm enthusiastically recommending it to family, friends and clients, for many types of losses!

- Kirk Richard Holt
author of "Nineteen Ways to Expand Your Potential"
Founder of Brighter Minds, LLC, www.brighterminds.co

Chapter 15 of Sheila Stephens' "Mystery School of Grief" was about my late wife, Dee's, passing over. Sheila wrote it beautifully. There is nothing I could add or change to make it better. It took me back to an understanding of "the Bridge" to the Other Side when Dee was crossing over, a very sad time for me but a joyous one for her. My eyes filled with tears as the memories flowed back to the last days of October and how Sheila comforted us all and ministered to Dee as she was crossing "the Bridge." I appreciate what Sheila wrote as I would not have remembered all the beauty of her passing. I would have remembered more of the emotional

loss and the grief. Now I have Chapter 15, "Bridges, Drumming, and Dee," and all the good Sheila brought to our family during such a hard time. I thank Sheila so much for this light-filled book.
    - Don Duncan

I feel there is a calmness that comes over me as I read through the chapters of "The Mystery School of Grief." As Sheila Stephens states when sharing the different ways to celebrate our Loved Ones, we let my late husband, Leroy's love flow through us in how we live our daily lives. In this way, we honor him as the life-force and the heart of our family. And during my hectic days, I am glad I can go back to many different chapters to re-read them.
    - Suzanne Hall

"Sheila Stephen's "The Mystery School of Grief, Healing Messages of Love & Light" truly reveals the deep understanding she has obtained through her own experiences of loss. It is real and raw, yet captivating. Throughout this book, love and compassion are gloriously illuminated. Your spirit simply cannot be anything but lifted when reading this book."
    -Samantha Gilbertson
    Pastoral Care, Mission Integration and Spiritual Care

The Mystery School
of Grief

Healing Messages of Love & Light

Sheila A Stephens

To Tricia,
thank you
for standing light
in the light

Sheila
Stephens

Flowers of the Spirit
Sherwood, Oregon

Flowers

of the Spirit™

"Humanity's Cares"
by Sheila Stephens

Pain walks in
and etches itself across my face.
"Don't you know, this isn't me?" I say.
"This is just temporary,"
and in one moment's breath, I realize
I am the Rembrandt's mirror of you -
the pain of all who have suffered.

At some time, my season of trials will be over,
or at least they may lessen into some new form of Grace,
so I may reclaim the spirit of me,
and I will show my face again,
but at that time it will be better -

a humble face, etched by the elements -
softened by humanity's cares,
more acutely aware
more compassionately aware
more kindly aware
of the Heart we all share.

Dedications

To Allen,
who still loves & guides me

To sons Jim & Julian,
my big-hearted heroes

Introduction

In the past ten years, since my husband Allen passed over, I've experienced some big ah-ha moments which I hope will illuminate your path in much the same ways they have mine. But I've also stumbled, had doubt, and have felt blocked. Healing from grief is often a bumpy road, so I want you to know I'm very human, and the big and small ah-ha moments were followed by my own inner work to bring the insights forward into my life. It's not helpful to put expectations on ourselves, or on life itself, to serve up extraordinary events. They will come when they will, especially if we have open hearts and minds.

We may find some momentous things happened, and we may have brushed them aside. So sometimes it's helpful to go back with new eyes and honor some of the nudges or serendipitous events we've experienced. When we're in the middle of the shock and chaos of grief, it's hard to find the quiet time we need in order to listen and assimilate the soft whispers of love being sent our way. We may also worry if we don't have some rather spectacular occurrences, but don't worry, both Spirit and the spirit of our Loved Ones will find a way to reach each of us - in a manner which is particularly our own. Our Loved Ones will reach us and continue to share their Love with us, but they don't interfere. We seem to have a natural privacy shield up that allows us to have our own lives when we want it, and this lets us live freely. But they are there when we need them, even when we don't realize it. I use the term Loved Ones (capitalized) to refer to them when they are on the Other Side. If it is not capitalized, it means our loved ones here, in our "regular" lives.

I call this book "The Mystery School of Grief" because grief has much to teach us if we gently turn toward the learning. It also opens us to many mysteries and amazing insights we wouldn't have had access to until we began this walk. But it is one of the hardest schools, and all of us who walk it are heroes. I wanted to share what I learned, and what has made my heart expand.

Along our walk, often our treasured insights come in bits and pieces. When you read the story of my direct experiences (instead of my assumptions), I hope you keep the long 10-year timeline in mind. It didn't come all at once, but I found the more I noticed, the more fluidly the healing insights came. Looking back now, I feel Spirit filled my life with talents, people, and experiences that would help me with this major life purpose, to help people heal from grief. I am deeply humbled and grateful.

I've drawn from a decade of my own dream journals, and have written my dreams out exactly as I wrote them down in the middle of the night or the dawn of early morning. I've also drawn from different spiritual traditions so people of all faiths and philosophies can feel comfortable as they fit it in with their own beliefs. It is my sincere hope this book will inspire you to find your own beautiful path of healing and peace. I've identified the wise people who spoke or wrote the various quotes that helped tell this expansive story, and if you find quotes without a name, they are my own.

This book is written for anyone who has loved deeply or has faced a big loss. I often say "There is no competition in grief; we need to treasure each person's needs to process strong feelings, even if they've lost someone they didn't have a good relationship with, as that unanswered potential is yet another kind of loss. My story is told from the perspective of a widow, but many things apply to all kinds of losses. It could be the loss of a treasured child, a close friend, a dear relative, or a sweet pet. The healing concepts also seem to help deal with a variety of losses, be it health, a job, or a relationship, etc.

I've capitalized the word Love when it applies to that bigger kind of Universal or Divine Love - the kind that is Unconditional, Wise, ever-Healing and Peace-filled. When we feel Centered and full of this kind of Love, it is Limitless. When that happens, we become the bigger versions of ourselves, and expand into the beautiful Lightness it brings.

May "The Mystery School of Grief; Healing Messages of Love & Light" bless you, comfort you, and let you know how much you are Loved. That is my greatest wish.

- Sheila Stephens

Table of Contents

Chapter One

Moving into the Higher Dimensions of Love

The thing I've learned about real Love, is that it never quits. Those who have loved us continue to love us on the Other Side. And they do so quite magnificently, if we let them. Each person we love is a blessing that changes us in untold ways, and we know our hearts are bigger, because of them. So even as we suffer and mourn, it is beneficial to stay open-hearted, and allow our hearts to become bigger yet, because of them. I've found that instead of thinking in terms of finality and "death," I think in terms of my Loved One's transcendence, surrounded by the amazing warmth and light of Unconditional Love. It's as if they are in a different neighborhood, but they like to send letters. If we think about the loving energy still sent by them, we open up our lives to more love, instead of less. And then what happens is quite miraculous. As for me, over the years my life became festooned with so many moments of love and insights from my late husband, Allen, and from Higher Spirit, that friends wanted me to share them, so others could walk in a softer path of healing.

From messages delivered by resplendent dragonflies and soaring hawks - to remarkable dreams, healings, stunning synchronicities, and remarkable occurrences - it seemed the Universe definitely wanted my attention. Staggeringly beautiful, and yet very practical, the things I learned were life-changing. I sometimes found them in my own Quiet Time as I opened my heart, but they very often came out of the blue, as sacred experiences, so I will share these experiences with you.

Looking back, it was an intense time, full of more dreams of love and guidance, and more Receiving than ever before in my life. The question was, "Would I keep my heart open to all the insights and wisdom being offered? Would I heal, because of Love?" I am glad I hung in there, and kept my eye on the sparrow, or in this case, the Red-Tailed Hawk and the light-filled Dragonfly.

It is tough though. When our Loved One passes over, we have a chance to either stop the flow of love, by whittling it down to a narrow trickle or a dried-up river bed of love, or to expand the flow of love by staying connected in a healthy way, and letting more love in. Amazingly, our Loved One will help us widen our path and show us how our days can be brightened with the gentle, but powerful energy of an ever-present love. Whether it is from our spouse, our child, a relative or a friend, this is a love that can tend us, and teach us for the rest of our lives. As we open to the awesome love from the Other Side, we will feel more love inside us.   We will also find ourselves standing, as if under a refreshing waterfall, in the Higher Dimensions of Love. These are doors of learning opened by our Loved One's passing over. Awkwardly, at first, I opened myself to this new path.

The turning point happened when I decided to let my Loved One's beauty shine through me - to touch those around me with this bounty of Love.   I am happy if others see Allen's love in my attitude and actions. For me, that decision alone watered the dry soil of my sorrow, and started me on a path of living vitally again, with my Loved One (and all he had to teach me) in my pocket. This book is written in honor of my dear Allen, who has helped me heal and live joyfully again.

This first chapter will give you concepts that form the foundation from which to begin, no matter what stage of grieving you are in, and then it's followed by many real stories from my life and my interior journey toward healing. Some are spectacular, some are funny, and some are just plain magical. I'll expand upon these concepts throughout this book, showing how they became pertinent in the ups and downs of my walk. I found these valuable nuggets could also be applied to life in general, so they stand amongst the highest on my list of gratitudes. They have profoundly helped me and those around me, so I hope they help you. Now it feels as if I stand in a broad, sunny meadow, so filled with the wildflowers of their gifts, they have to be shared. It's like walking around with a huge, overflowing bouquet. You can't keep it all to yourself.

I call the process of grieving a Mystery School because in all the Mystery Schools of life, something is learned. It may be learned by having goals and manifesting your highest thoughts (such as in the popular book, "The Secret"). It may be by learning about healing; or by learning how to fight through obstacles, etc. There are myriad forms of Mystery Schools, but all of them are really based on actual life, and the wisdoms gained are meant to be used in our real lives. One of the hardest of those Schools, in my opinion, is what I call the Mystery School of Grief. It is one of the most painful, and not one any of us want to volunteer to endure. All of these true Mystery Schools, these walks of wisdom, are spiritual in nature, as they ask you to go beyond what seems real, into a deeper level of learning and existence, so you may, in your own way, be transformed and your spirit may expand.

In this way, we enter into our own kind of Transcendence. Before, it was above our pay grade, so to speak. But now, during grief, we are presented with the epic opportunity for our own spirit to learn, grow and then give more spaciously. Sounds quite remarkable, and it is - but it can happen a bit at a time, and seems to go at the pace that allows us time to internalize it.

If we take our journey of grieving as a serious path of learning, we may find opportunity during crisis, and even as we fall apart, we may find a new part of our being come into life. And we may find the Divine Source always there, sending Love and Wisdom through the hearts of our Loved Ones - straight into ours.

Since the caring but dynamic Mystery School of Grief wants to get started, with concepts you can use for the rest of your life, let's dive right in.

To honor our Loved Ones and begin the path to authentic healing, it benefitted me to think about something basic and vital. I was inspired to think about how:

All grief begins with Love.

Because the energy of Love is an Eternal Gift,
Love can Grow after our loss.

It makes sense that all grief begins with love, for we would have no sorrow, without love for the person who has passed. We would have no joys, without love for the people and passions in our lives. And if all the scientists in all the Universe could eventually find the Source of all things, I propose that Source would be the magnificent energy of Love. So we benefit greatly by taking that Love into our process of grieving. Again and again, as I read my notes written years ago in my journals, I saw Allen's "angel-words" of guidance:

Begin with Love.

Isn't that a beautiful thing for your Loved One to tell you? To begin with love. It still works its magic in my heart.

This foundational concept is very pivotal, since during grief, many other feelings are vying for top billing of our emotions, of course, and they are not invalid feelings. And we need to feel what we feel. We may feel devastated, anxious, or sad beyond words. We may feel angry, guilty or frustrated. We may feel exhausted, hollowed-out, or even temporarily relieved, especially after seeing someone through a long-term illness. We may feel as if we are caught in a fog, or we may attempt to stuff our feelings, only to see them come out in assorted ways as we cut off part of our emotional life. We may find ourselves feeling fearful, resentful, withdrawn, or totally stagnated. We may feel all of these things, and at different times. The stages of grief often go back and forth and catch us by surprise. And before long, we may find ourselves far away from the source of Love that moves the Universe, and moves us. At some point we may yearn for a kind of balance that only comes from within. But how do we find it without our Loved One's physical presence in our lives? We begin by actively but gently stepping into the Mysteries.

Secret Number 1:
Become a gentle Avatar of Love.
Because grief begins with love, and is based on love,
then Love is the foundation, the guiding force of healing.

If we start there, in love's domain,
and decide to give it our attention,
and let it multiply instead of decrease,
our grief will be filled, more and more,
with a healing kind of grace -

because Love is being activated.

Thankfully, this is not a grace we have to manufacture. Instead, it's a kind of grace that blooms within us as we follow love. It's the kind of grace that makes us a bigger person, bringing us gifts of understanding - big insights we'll want to share with others. But this path requests our focus. First of all, it asks us to Notice Love: Love from your Loved One, and from the Higher Spirit that moves in all things, however you might define that. In the midst of our grief, this may feel like a tall order, but one of the secrets is to open your heart to your Loved One, and keep it open - not in a tense way, but in a balanced, free-flowing way. As you do, you will naturally receive love in many remarkable ways. And as you walk in this Light, you will become a gentle Avatar, on a brave mission filled with an heroic kind of love. And *if you stumble and get off track, you can center yourself again - by beginning again, with Love.*

I think about the great question my friend, Dave Davenport, posses to himself, "What can I do today that my future self will hug me for?" And I also add, "What can I do today that my Loved One on the Other Side will hug me for?" What kinds of things will each of us choose to do? Large or small, these intention-filled actions hold tremendous healing power, and they are some of the first ways we can honor the transcendent path that wants us to multiply Love. I reflected Allen's love by taking little steps and eventually edited and produced his Western book of fiction, "Gone to Glory," during the first year after his passing. It was a great way of celebrating him - and it made me feel good. It gave me many small but loving steps to take, and it kept me in a loving space. One mom, after her daughters were killed by a vehicle, continued making and giving out an item her daughters had begun making - an item with a heart on it. Now they are all over the world. And some other parents chose to make a colorful flower garden at their elementary school, in honor of their daughter. All these things count, for they are forces for good, and they contain the energy of your Loved One - and you - still together on a path.

This new reality - of the expansive dimension of Love - helps us heal. As I watched her TV interview, the young mother's voice changed as she got into her story. It changed from trembling with sorrow, to open and confidant expressions of Love as she concentrated on sharing her daughters' "hearts" with other people who need them in the here and now. Before my eyes, she became an Avatar of Love. I admired her, and I also immediately felt the great hearts of her loving daughters.

Like the young mom, I, too, felt my sorrow lift when I connected with Allen's buoyant spirit in a project. I enjoyed editing and then sharing Allen's beautiful book of adventure and deeper learning with people whose lives he had touched on his large Schwan's food delivery route in Hillsboro. I savored touching each word he had so daringly written, and it strikes me now how both of us were being Avatars of Love in this joint project. In fact, by doing this inspired project, I was actually helping Allen's spirit express itself and continue to be an active Avatar of Love. I'm sure he's busy doing many vital things on the Other Side, but our connection with our Loved Ones offers another avenue for their love to make a difference. Doing this made a great difference to me, and then quite quickly, to others. The memories of the happy smiles and loving hugs at the book signing party our sons and I held in honor of Allen a year after his passing still makes me happy - and very fulfilled. And friends were able to take Allen's spirit home - in their pockets!

Small things can make a big difference. Maybe it's something you do for yourself, or something nice someone else has done for you, and maybe you continue it. I remember receiving a small thing with a big impact. When I was grieving, I received a beautiful, hand-knitted Angel for Hope in the mail, not once, but twice - from two anonymous people. (The enclosed note from Angels for Hope said: "Someone special has requested that you receive this 'Angel for Hope' so that you would know that you are loved and cared about. Our thoughts and prayers are with you." These acts of compassion still comfort me. I finally was able to give one Angel away to another friend in need, but I kept the other Angel. Even a decade later, it hangs on my wall calendar, near me in my office.

Receiving those thoughtful gifts, just out-of-the-blue, made me want to give back in honor of Allen, so even though the Angels are free (you just provide the name and address you want to send it to, and whether you want it to be anonymous or in your name), I donated to the nonprofit group that makes them, so the volunteer knitters could have the yarn they needed to keep up the good work. In fact, I think I'll do so again. You can give any amount, and you can look up groups like this on the internet. (See: *Angelsforhope.org* which is active at this time.)

My neighbor's family also did something wonderful like this to honor unborn children. The parents, John and Jenna, who lost their first born son, said they "learned that very small things which seem unimportant to others, mean a great deal to us."

During their years of healing, the family's good friend, Annie, developed a charity to send out beautiful, tiny "Calvin Hats," knitted with Love by volunteers. At one time Johns Hopkins was ordering boxes and boxes of them, so they went out worldwide. Even though this is no longer active, even hearing about it affects my heart. Imagine how much healing occurred when families received these tiny knitted caps of Love in the mail! Calvin surely became an angel, in so many ways!

Several days ago, I asked the grandmother of Calvin how many grandchildren she had. She so beautifully said, "Eight. One of them is on the Other Side, so we have 7 here." I liked the fact that Barb still counted 8.

In all these simple ways of honoring our Loved Ones, the gentle Avatar of Love in you starts practicing how to live a bigger life - not a smaller one - because of your Loved One. In many ways, we learn:

Secret Number 2:
Don't Let Your Loved One Go,
Let Your Loved One In.

Other acts of practicing this energy-changing lovingkindness can be as simple as calling a friend, or taking care of a pet. What makes it special is the Love you put into it, in honor of the one who has passed over. It affirms how your Loved One's spirit is still alive in your heart. In my experience, your Loved One rejoices as you let his or her spirit inspire you. You can feel love multiply, as your spirit aligns with their love. If your son loved dogs, you could volunteer or donate to a pet rescue center. If your husband liked to write, you could teach a writing workshop for kids, in honor of him. If your friend enjoyed fishing, you could take a senior or a youngster fishing. These simple acts hold enormous healing energy, because they start recapturing and catalyzing a purposeful life within you - a life based on the ongoing exchange of love, and that is some of the best medicine for us. If we stand in the mix of love, some good love is bound to be stirred up!

Sometimes, during grief, it is hard to "get ourselves out - into the mix." But this "celebrating-love" way of thinking will ease your way. As you find your own ways to celebrate and honor your Loved One, the Grace we talked about will enter in, and it will help you. For many people, and at many times in our lives, the ability to stay "in the mix" of life is huge. True healing comes not only from staying connected to your Loved One's spirit in a balanced way, but bringing that love into real life. When we "let our Loved Ones in," instead of "letting them go," their spirit can join us in adding more Love to our lives. So instead of "moving on," let's allow their love to move into us and through us, into all the people and purposes that call our names.

Secret Number 3:
Love has the Greatest Energy.

*In the Energy is the Gift -
to help you
Become More, because of Love.*

If we think about it, Love has the greatest energy. It is the dynamo capable of moving mountains within us. It is the Great Teacher that awakens us and connects us to something greater than ourselves. And when we turn toward it, it has the power, the

Quantum Force to make us our best selves through any walk in life, including the Mystery School of Grief. During grief, we may be tempted to turn off Love, but it is so damaging to do so, as it hurts both you and the people around you. When we block love, we stop these small, potent ways of giving, and in a daily life kind of way, we stop celebrating our Loved One. We can all too easily be caught in misery instead. For these reasons, as soon as we can, it is good to find a kind-hearted antidote to becoming stuck in the destructive kind of grief. One-step-at-a-time, we can claim Love.

So when we start intentionally focusing on the great gifts our Loved One brought us, we start Noticing Love. In that moment, we start harmonizing with it. This is a pivotal act which releases a powerful flow of Energy. Much like a well-thought-out karate kick, the act of Noticing points us to more Love, both from your Loved One and from the Divine - and how its many healing forms are present in our lives. When you start noticing, it can really surprise you. *As for me, I am amazed how the Great Spirit of Love, itself, steps up without a moment of hesitation and volunteers to help us walk through grief's doors, so we won't get permanently stuck in our authentic tears and real-life pain.* In my experience, as we sincerely grieve, Love will hold our hand, and - with our consent - teach us how to thrive again - this time, maybe in a different way. I will soon tell you many real-life stories of my own experiences, and of my own first steps into higher dimensions of Love - how Spirit touched my shoulder, and gave me a gift that helped me understand *I could heal, and become More - because of Love.*

This is how it began, how it prepared my heart.

Chapter Two

Feeling the Miraculous, through the Beauty of the Open Heart

*There are moments during grief
when a window is opened into the beyond,
and we are allowed to experience
the Miraculous power & presence of Love.*

*These moments, if appreciated & remembered,
will stay with us for the rest of our lives.
They are Love's Way of holding our hand
and guiding us tenderly.*

As I mentioned, I found the term "death" didn't fit my experience, for Love is not finite, but is rather a power that fills your heart, wherever you are. So when someone passes through the Veil to the Other Side, it's the quintessential time to pay attention and stand close to the meteor shower. When someone passes over, and at many times after that major event, we can enter the Miraculous - as we stop and take some sacred time just to *feel Love, both from our Loved One and from the Divine.* The feeling of the Miraculous qualities of Love may sweep into the inner chambers of our hearts in our quiet time, while talking with friends, or at a Celebration of Life, for instance.

As we stop the busy-ness of our common days, so naturally strewn with jobs and duties, schedules and demands, many of us suddenly realize, more than ever before, how valuable love is, and how valuable that particular person's love was and is! We feel what a difference the love from one person can make! This is one of the reasons Celebrations of Life are important. In those timeless moments, we open our hearts, and, in a revealing kind of way, we experience Love - the sacred depth and breadth of Love. On the deepest of levels, we *appreciate* Love.

This, itself, is a Miracle. To actually feel Love, and the affect it has on our lives, is momentous. So we shouldn't just skip over these moments that fill us with our Loved One's light.

As we stop the world for a while, and stand in Love's Domain - we feel the powerful happiness someone's love can bring to us. We feel it like the warmth of the Sun, or the essence of a radiant yellow Rose opening its petals in the generous light of summer. This alone can change us, as we value it, and decide to let it tend us and guide us in our coming days. In a moment of the Miraculous, we can decide to "pay it forward" and let our Loved One's legacy be activated within our own lives, here and now. With these few steps, the gentle Avatar in us steps forward with Love. The Avatar now has a path. And this Higher Path immediately but gently begins filling with the soft, healing energy that will help someone else you know, and others you may never know. The healing effect goes out in ripples, far beyond our own known sphere.

And so, *we begin with Love.* As we stand within its warm energies, our heart opens to understand the mysteries. Our experience with Love begins to guide us to know for ourselves. Even as we suffer during this life-altering time after a Loved One passes over, we find ourselves reaching out with questions and an awakened desire to understand what is happening - and what is beyond the Veil. How do Life and "Death" fit together? And where are we in all of this? Confusion seeks illumination, possibly more than any other time in our lives.

Intuitively, and because of feeling some of the Miraculous dimensions of Love, I think we understand there is something of portent near at hand, some great potential that exists within us and within this situation - a potential capable of changing even the energetic dimensions of our heart. We might liken this to "sacred geometry," (which deals with forms and energy), when the very form of grief allows for the expansion of the heart in a way no other time does. (Sacred geometry is considered to be universal patterns naturally occurring in every thing in our reality.)

Since we are always in a creative state (whether consciously or unconsciously), and always making ourselves anew as we merge with our experiences to grow - this pivotal period of time of grief offers more possibilities for change and expansion than almost any other life event.   It offers the incredible opportunity to increase the dimensions, compassion, and capacity of our hearts!

At a talk recently, the speaker said, "The body is made up of electricity. The head has many electrical impulses, but the etheric heart has 3,000 times more!" So healing comes more rapidly and naturally when we tend to our hearts.

How we take our journey will determine if our spirit shrivels up or expands, so it is highly important, not only to us, but to the Universe as a whole, that we care for our spirit and encourage it to become more instead of less as we honestly grieve. A crucial part of taking care of ourselves is to allow our own spirit to be tended by Spirit. In this way of Allowing, and Letting in More, The Mystery School of Grief wants to teach us a priceless secret:

Secret Number 4:
Open your heart; don't close it.

Grief is a process
meant to Open our hearts,
not close them.

So hang on, hang on. Hang on to your open heart. I know it is breaking, but through your own work with Love, your heart can break *open,* allowing unexpected beauty to enter in. And the new form (of what you learn and who you become in your life) can feel as breathtaking as sacred geometry. Or a new star in the heavens.

I never knew then what I would know now - that, even 10 years after my husband, Allen, passed over, I would love him so much more. And I had loved him with my whole heart then. To my surprise, I have experienced more love, and ever more love, not only for Allen, but for those around me and for life itself during this challenging time of change. I am grateful Allen has helped me every step of the way.

Socially, we have been taught to die a bit, or a lot, when someone we love dies. It is usually considered only "a loss" at the table of win or lose. But what if, instead, we open our hearts to this new kind of relationship - one in which we could keep learning and growing with our Loved One. Even *because* of our Loved One.

Secret Number 5:
The Energy of Love,
(from one heart to another)
can cross the Barriers of Time and Space.

Because Love is an energy, an ever-lasting energy, it never leaves us. It can jump tall buildings. It can whisper your name and find you in a dream. And it can encourage you from the Other Side of the Veil. Think of this: when your Loved One was alive, did you love your Loved One any less when you closed your eyes? Or when he or she went to work? Or when your Loved One sent you a hug over the phone?

Of course not - because *Love is an energy. It crosses the barriers of time and space.* We can feel it even when our Loved One is not physically with us. So it is no wonder Love passes through another unseen barrier. And *as Love passes through the Veil between what we call Life and "Death," Love does an incredible thing:*

Love multiplies.

It can multiply within us. It can even multiply within our Loved One on the Other Side. And the most beautiful thing is this Love - which is both born *of* us, and is *with* us - can be shared - so it multiplies yet again, and again.

As I've said, the beauty of this advanced kind of Love can especially be won while walking through The Mystery School of Grief. It begins by opening ourselves up to the possibilities of Love without boundaries of time or space.

"Love is the Emissary to the Other Side"

But I didn't know all these things in the beginning. When Allen passed over, it was like a ship had left and I wasn't on it. My life changed almost completely overnight, and often I felt adrift, and rudderless. It would take me time and experience to figure out my path - but this is a valuable part of the process. I had times of both opening my heart, and shutting my heart. During those times, I both opened and shut my life, but I learned from it all.

As I learned from the beginning, there is no perfect way through grief, but the key is to keep going on your journey, like you're hiking to an incredible lake. You may get tired along the way, but the lake is a jewel, and you don't want to turn back and miss seeing it. You also don't realize how much you are watched over and cared for as you hike this path - this sacred Journey of Love. If only I knew the riches I would receive, I would have faced forward sooner, or more often. I would have been wiser. I would have gotten stuck less often. But each footstep of my inner journey in this Mystery School of Grief left me not perfect, but more perfected by Love - a Love that although invisible, crosses the barriers of time and space, and permeates everything. It could permeate my heart, if only I let it, and that's what happened in my first Moments of Grace.

Chapter Three

The First Steps:
Moments of Grace

In the midst of grief, I had "Moments of Grace," as I call them now. They started one by one, then multiplied. They multiplied so much that people wanted me to write them down, so they could see all of them, the whole picture. Like jewels on a necklace. Or like stepping stones on a path that brings you home. Each one brought a moment of Peace - a moment of Peace that would last a lifetime. I always knew it when they happened. Each one brought a revealing. A deep understanding. A wisdom that went far beyond ordinary living.

Secret Number 6:
Treasure Moments of Grace

These Moments of Grace are meant to be treasured, but even the best of us can brush them off, and dishonor the enormity of the gift we have been offered from Spirit. So Moments of Grace will come, but our response to them is the gift we give back to Spirit. If we really notice them, take them in, and then keep them in our heart, so we can remember them whenever we need their wisdom and reassurance, then we've shown our gratitude for these small and large miraculous moments.

The first Moment of Grace for me began at Allen's passing. The event itself was a full-flung shock. He was hit and killed by someone driving a truck in a school zone. Standing by the driver's door of his Schwan's food delivery truck, my tender, handsome, generous-hearted Allen died in the short but long minutes that followed. He died without the comfort of my hand holding his, or the presence of myself and our two fine sons surrounding him with our love. He was happy, vital, and so loving. He was just 57. Before the joys of retirement could be shared. Before we could relax after all the efforts of work, home, and raising our family.

Even today, writing this still makes me bump up against my tears. They still take me unaware, like something that jumps into view as you round the corner. It is true, I lost many things that day. I don't hide those losses, and there will always be tears unshed. *I think I shall only shed the last of my tears as I pass over, and give them into the arms of Divine Spirit, who knows the depth and breadth of my love.*

Still, I was helped immediately. I didn't learn of Allen's passing all at once. When it happened, I was out on errands. I still think back to how I was forewarned. As I parked in a lot, ready to go in and get a new stereo Allen liked, my spirit suddenly came to a cosmic stop. At the same moment, while I was starting to call my son at home, I heard a siren. I had just become seriously concerned, as Allen hadn't returned my cell phone calls that morning, and he was always calling me. Looking back, I now believe Spirit sent some "messengers" to ease my way, and ease the shock.

Not one emergency vehicle, but three went past me - an ambulance, then another ambulance, and then a firetruck flew past, one after the other - their horns blaring. As I understand synchronicities, I was immediately alert. Then my kind, adult son, Jim, (who I believe was also placed there as my angel) was on the phone with me.

The twenty-minute drive home was an agony, an endurance test, and I knew from Jim that the police had come to my house. They didn't want to talk to me on the phone; they would talk to me when I arrived.

Bad sign.

When I walked in the door, escorted by Jim (who had met me on the front walk outside), I heard the actual, life-splitting words that Allen had been hit and killed by a truck, near a quiet, residential school zone on a sunny blue-sky October day.

There is no way to write this without still feeling the shock and pain of those moments in that day. I was so thankful my loving son was with me! Together we sat down and held hands to hear the words he'd already heard, but now would reach my ears. But as I sat down to listen to the police officer and the chaplain who had been sent to inform me, something quite surprising happened. Always close as close with my sweet husband of 23 years, I felt a moment in time that has become priceless to me. I felt my heart steadily open - not to the new people in the room, or their particular words of explanation and kind condolence. Instead, it opened to Allen. And it opened to the Miraculous. It sat on my shoulder and informed me right then and there, and for many days afterward. It was a deep, abiding feeling, and a vision all in one. In the moments before the two well-meaning men left (and then again afterward, when I was alone with my tears), I felt an incredible Peace flow into me.

I often remember one great feeling. I remember the absolute feeling of Allen's soul expanding, as he transcended into the spacious arms of Divine Love. I still cry at feeling this. And I was and am happy for Allen. Really, what a sacred event! All too often, in our own shock and grief, we pass over this miraculous occurrence, but if we take an in-breath moment, and let ourselves connect, not with what we see on the earth plane, but instead with the spirit of our Loved One when we learn he or she has passed over - ahhhh, what a transcendent moment it is. For spirit, what a beautiful, beautiful moment. So it was that I was able to spend some time feeling this luminous moment, both for Allen and now for me, before other realities set in. (This was miraculous, even though Allen died in an accident. I have been told that Allen left his body before his death. This grace and spiritual protection happens during many accidents or even during other violent events and deaths. This knowledge helped me immensely, and I was told this about Allen's passing from different sources.)

So it was, in these first moments of actually knowing Allen had passed over, I felt all the love I had for Allen, and for Allen's great journey, both here, and on his way to the Other Side. As I felt time "Condense into the All," I felt my beloved's life-time, and the grand, whole-hearted celebration of who he was, and what an impact he'd had on me - and as I would learn, on so many others in his life. I still feel such peace when I think of those moments of enlightened clarity for me, when I felt I stood within the stars, and understood them.

I felt my dear Allen. His spirit - so light, and real, and glowing.

And I felt his spirit lift.

I felt his spirit lift into the arms of an unconditional Love so warm and beautiful that, by proxy, it made me feel good.

Amazingly, I felt Allen go Home . . .

It was a moment to me that was golden. He was surrounded by a Love that made my eyes overflow with good tears. And I felt happy for my dear Allen.

Standing in my living room that afternoon, and as I escorted the local policeman and the chaplain out; then later, sitting in bed that night; and then again, when I put my head on the pillow and had a chat with Allen before sleep - I celebrated Allen's wonderful going Home. At that time, I was able to think of Allen, instead of just myself. And because I had allowed my heart to open to him, I had felt and could still feel his incredible lightness of being. He had not wanted to leave me, but he was happy. And he was sharing that happiness with me. Showing me what it would be like.

I felt illuminated. And at peace. *Like I understood something I never wanted to forget.*

It filled my heart with a huge, boundless gift of Love that can only be felt when someone you deeply love passes over. It might be a spouse or a parent, a child, a relative, or a dear friend. Even a special pet. The depth of your love for them seems to direct your heart to open.

I still thank my Allen for that feeling and that vision.

And I still thank Divine Spirit for that, too.

I had just experienced a Love that encompasses all of us. It must be like what many people must feel in a near-death experience. The quality of unconditional Love you receive when something like this happens to you feels too life-changing not to be shared. The Love from it bubbles up inside you and overflows. You want everyone to know how good it feels.

This is hard to write, to translate into words, for it is such big stuff. But during grief, other people have experiences like this quite often. We understand. And for a moment, we stand there, in the Miraculous, with them.

I vowed to stay in this higher state of understanding, and I did for a while. But then life bonked me on the head sometime after Allen's Celebration of Life ceremony, and I realized I would have to work to regain this state of illumination. I would need many reminders.

But I had experienced a Moment of Grace. And that made all the difference.

Looking back, I realize that even during the shock and first stages of grief:

> ** I had experienced and felt Love - the big Love that guides us all*
> ** I had felt Allen's love as an Energy that would stay with me*
> ** I had kept my heart open and had started Receiving*
> ** I had been comforted by Allen's presence, on the Other Side*

As I looked at it, I realized I had glimpsed across the Veil, with Allen's spirit of love holding my hand! Now that was a new one! Maybe I should keep Noticing Love - however it came.

After I wrote this chapter, I went out to dinner to relax with a friend. A bright penny flashed and caught my eye (more about "Pennies from Heaven" in Chapter 7), and as I bent to pick it up, I realized it definitely wasn't on the front floor of my car a few hours earlier. And in the garage, there wasn't even any sunlight to make it flash. Then, as we drove through town, a rare firetruck passed by. This time, the sirens weren't blaring.

The first night of Allen's death, I went to bed, and settled in to be close to his spirit. That night, in my quiet time, I asked questions I had never asked before. I never thought they would be answered on the delicate but deceptively strong wings of an iridescent blue dragonfly . . .

Chapter Four

On the Wings of Love

Quietly closing the door to my room, I let out a deep breath, and then took in an even deeper breath. Finally, I was alone enough just to *be* with Allen, even if he was in spirit. I just wanted to feel him around me, which I did. Love will do that for you - indeed, it is there, like the greatest forces of nature, maybe unseen but powerful. In those moments of tangibly feeling Allen's love, even after his passing, I felt more deeply than before, how -

"Love is a real thing."

In that centered place, I did my first wise thing. I silently asked, *"Allen, how will I know you're with me?"* And I opened up my mind a bit in his direction. "Will it be a butterfly?" . . . "No, that's me." Then in a flash, "Oh, it'll be a dragonfly! You've been talking about them all these months." We'd watched them on our deck, as they visited us all summer and into the fall.

And so it was, that in the stillness of the night, I felt Allen's spirit helping me. In only a few short moments, a natural pathway for our communication had opened up. It felt right, and my body relaxed. Even though I remember and work with my dreams, I had no dream that night, nor would I for quite some time. Now I would have to start a new walk, without Allen physically at my side - and sometimes not even in my dreams.

The next day broke with sunshine and a warm but slightly crisp October day. When summer lingers into fall, we call it an Indian Summer here in the Northwest. As Jim had been living with us then, healing from a long-term illness, we went out together for some fresh air. Upon returning home, we walked up to our front door, a door that looked a bit forlorn without Allen's presence in our home. Head down, I was fetching my keys, and behind me a step, Jim was free to look about.

"Mom, something just buzzed me! "

I wondered if it was a hornet. As I turned around to look, prepared to deflect a potential sting, I stopped in my tracks. Together we both looked at what had just buzzed him, but was now flittering about us with the lightest of wings, as though it was dancing into our sphere. Taking its time. Wanting to announce its presence. Wanting to say hello and visit - like it had all the time in the world, and wanted to settle in for a chat. Our eyes were instantly glued on our visitor.

"Oh my God, it's a dragonfly!" I quietly exclaimed, stunned by its presence.

"Mom, it's a dragonfly!" Jim said at almost the same time.

Our mutual pronouncements cut through the air, just like the beautiful dragonfly wings were cutting through the air of our grief. As it dawned on both of us that, "Yes, it was a dragonfly!" - the whole tone of our morning lifted, and we had soft giggles in our hearts. We could hardly believe it, yet here it was, announcing itself. Announcing itself on the first day possible.

I blinked back tears of appreciation. They were tears that knew, "Yes, love is real."

I would remember this gift from Allen's spirit almost everyday I came up the walk to our home. It opened my heart to Love's devotion and determination from across the Veil. And it came to my son, and then to me, on the soft but strong wings of an iridescent blue dragonfly. To my ongoing delight, it was the first in a whole host of dragonfly visitations over the years. Even 10 years later, we still receive "visits."

After that, Jim and I behaved differently. We went inside and realized we now thought a bit differently. We had experienced a miracle, and I realized I was glad for the questions I'd asked about how Allen would show us when he was near, so I hope you will ask your Loved One the same question: "How will you let me know your spirit is nearby?" Many people receive answers such as rainbows, and light-winged butterflies, etc. It is all quite beautiful. It is also very personal and unique. As I was talking with my close friend, Suzanne, recently, she asked the same question.   I immediately felt the answer from her dear Leroy was "Lifeforce." Over the last two years, I could see Leroy's beautiful Lifeforce come to Suzanne, and pour out in loving, helpful ways to inspire the whole family. I loved what I saw. This also underlines how each of us may feel our Loved Ones spirit in very different ways, so it is important not to judge, nor expect it to come in a certain way.   As I began loving the vulnerable but strong wings of the dragonflies who found their way to me, I also found the warmth of Allen's spirit deep in my heart had the same beauty I needed.   All of this was something I could share, as the miracle of Love was magnified, even through the Veil.

Now, step by step, even though I was stumbling my way into it, I was quickly being taught how to live in a way in which miracles can happen.

Secret Number 7:
Lift your head & eyes upward,
and Ask Questions that have the same Positive Direction.
What can I Learn & how can I Grow?

Questions are good - especially if they are oriented in a positive direction. In life, we are constantly pointing ourselves in a direction. If we practice mindfulness during this time of grief, we can actually point ourselves toward healing if we start with great questions. The question, "Why me?" is destined to torture and depress us. Some people counter with the question, "Why not me?" - for *all* of us face the challenges brought by loss. But the question, "What can I learn and how can I grow?" will expand the possibilities for understanding and expanding our own spirit.

Sometimes, in our sorrow, we find ourselves going around with our heads down. When I wrote about this real incident with the first dragonfly visitation, I realized how symbolic it was that I had my head and eyes down when I was seeking to open the front door. In much of grieving, that can all too easily be the case. But Jim had his head up, and he was able to see the visit from the dragonfly first, from the very beginning.

Spirit had given me a clue. Well, two clues. In my first steps of being a courageous Avatar of Love, I had: 1) asked a good question (and it had been answered); and 2) now I realized the power in paying attention, even in being ready, so I wouldn't miss these touches from Heaven. I wanted to lift my head and eyes up, so I could see the Answers when they came. I didn't want to miss a thing.

As I write this, I see yet another layer of healing that came via the gossamer-winged dragonfly. When it visited us, it was in the same place where Jim had helped me walk to our front door just before I heard the crushing words of Allen's passing. By changing a painful place that had a bad memory, into a place that now contains a good memory, Allen took another burden off my shoulders. I am amazed how his caring spirit continues my healing, even now.

These ongoing gifts from our Loved Ones on the Other Side can stun us with their beauty. Doesn't this decision (to lift our heads up in order to see God's possibilities) also apply to life in general? The secret wisdoms we learn in this Mystery School of Grief go far beyond grief's sphere, but are revealed within this walk. It opens our hearts to accept even more Love than before.

Secret Number 8:
Receive a new Lightness of Love
from the ways your Loved One communicates with you,
as he or she reflects the Ongoing Love from the Divine.

Once you've been hit by a megadose of Love from the Other Side, you have the motivation to pay attention to this new form of communicating. I strongly feel Higher Spirit is teaching us more about Love by infusing our Loved Ones with ways to inspire us, for Love is meant to be shared. In this way, it is NOT a parlor game. Rather, it is a sacred journey into a Light so bright it can heal us from within. So to be given an opportunity to let Higher Spirit into the process, and then to receive a new Lightness of Love from the Other Side is an opportunity to learn how to live with that Light in the here and now.

It is also an opportunity for our Loved Ones. Author John Edwards talks about how *our Loved Ones on the Other Side are given an important Assignment - to help the people they love.*

Imagine what kind of grade they would get on their assignments if we ignore their helpful ways! If we turn our backs and discount their messages of Love, we do both ourselves, and them, a great disservice.

It is different though.   Just as the dragonfly's actual occurrence surprised Jim and myself, this new form of communication takes some adjustment. But when it happens so beautifully, in your heart you know it is a miracle you need to accept and honor. As you pay attention to it, you pave the pathway for it to happen again. Many people who say this doesn't happen to them are blocking it, or discounting these loving missives.   To help it happen more often, we need to remember we are one-half of the communication. Our Loved Ones rejoice when we pick up the mail, and send a figurative thank you note their way. This is a new form of sacred practice, and they rejoice because we are being harmonious with a deeper layer of Love - a Love that doesn't stop, but only grows, on the Other Side of the Veil.

One of the most beautiful things I've learned is how these gifted moments from my Loved One often come when I'm in need. I don't look for Allen, but he appears in some form most often when I am worried or overwhelmed. In this way, we are reminded again and again of Compassion. For me, it underlines the feeling I am never alone. This can change our life-view, and knowing we're not alone can change the whole way we grieve.

It can lighten us up a bit, and give us dragonfly wings when we truly need them.

Secret Number 9:
Joy and Pain
can sit side by side.

Understand the Yin Yang of Opposites,
Use the Wisdom of Balance
to create a Healing Circle within yourself.

At this moment, I just looked down at my watch, only to find I've slipped it on upside down! That's opposites, all right! And that's how Spirit talks to you after a while; Spirit meets you where you're at and guides you - sometimes even makes you laugh.

I've found that most of all, Spirit wants to help us find Balance because it's the place where we can heal and where we can create. A good symbol of Balance is captured within the ancient Yin Yang symbol, wherein two opposites are brought together into a circle. One of the keys to processing our grief is to recognize and use these opposites wisely. Together the two opposites form a Balance Circle that enables us to get through things by understanding the interplay of these opposites, so simply knowing these two opposites exist brings wisdom. They may tell us how the opposites of Pain and Joy can sit side by side, for instance. This speaks of how we sometimes need to experience the Joys of the present, and take breaks from our grief. We need to breathe, take a walk in the sunshine, and laugh with friends. By thinking in terms of opposites, we can understand how OK that is, even how healthy it is. It makes us understand how we shouldn't feel guilty when, during our long journey of grieving, we have times of feeling good.

It also connotes the vision of how Joy may come in the morning. That "morning" may come in little moments at first, but it is the spark of life, and that spark of life is from the Lifeforce of Spirit, so we don't always have to feel sad at every moment to "prove" our love for someone who's passed over. Quite the contrary, eventually the wisest goal, and the point of the Balance Circle, is to get us to the place where we show our love through the beautiful way we celebrate our Loved One in our day to day life. *We get to the place of Balance and Peace by honoring all our feelings, both Pain and Joy. The Pain can actually lead us to the Joy wanting to break through. It begins in small ways, like crocus breaking through winter's ways to show us spring.*

One acquaintance talked to me two months after Allen's passing, and I said I was kind of tired of feeling sad, and was ready to talk about other things at times. But, maybe because she didn't understand these dichotomies, or because I didn't express myself well, she sent a heavy bundle of guilt my way - and then, you bet, I felt worse!

At the same time, the second Christmas after Allen's passing, the opposite happened - I fell to my knees with a sudden, deep sorrow at the loss of my dear love. I was around some people who didn't want to listen or help me through that piercing sorrow when it came out, so it increased my pain. When we are not allowed to express these deeply held feelings when they want to come out, it can thwart our progress. Healing from grief is a bumpy path, full of totally opposite feelings. It is a great lesson to take it as it comes - both the Pain and the Joy. We need to do that for ourselves, and the people around us can help by doing the same thing. If friends just check in with us by asking, "How are you feeling today?" - it opens up a genuine, helpful conversation.

You'll notice the Yin Yang symbol has a circle around it. When we honor our feelings and process them in a healthy way, we start that circle moving. Our feelings are not stuck, but both are duly noted, and given room to breathe. When Pain and Joy can sit side by side, we give ourselves the gift of release - and the space to heal. So as we begin to recognize the power of Opposites, we begin to make choices that improve our mental health. We can see what we need, and when - and we can tend ourselves. This develops self-love and self-respect, and eventually, even as we experience the pain of grief, allows us to make room for something higher to come in. It is then, in this Healing Circle, we open ourselves to a new kind of Love that creates an energy of movement in our lives.

If you are human, like I definitely am, you'll find yourself experiencing both sides of the coin. As for pain, the most helpful words of healing for me have been:

"Jesus wept."
John 11:35

These two words have eased my pain again and again, because they shared the burden of my pain. I can't tell you how many times I thought of these sacred words, and each time I felt comforted beyond measure.

Years later, I was also moved by the creative power of Dreamtime in the Australian aboriginal culture:

In a dream, I was told, and was shown how:

"We weave our new world into existence, together."

I watched as the Australian aborigines (and myself) took beautiful brightly colored pieces of cloth - which are our dreams - and played drums and music and danced, while we wove a new world into existence - together. These worlds are from our dreams, and they also ARE our dreams.

Within each Opposite is a key: even as we experience Chaos, we may find Peace. And even what we thought of as Truth can become a New kind of Truth. That New Truth may start with the physical truth of This Side, and open up to the new vistas from the Other Side. When we gain wisdom from Opposites, we may open our hearts to receive a healing force within our situation. As Jim and I met the dragonfly at our front door, we had both felt our hearts uplifted. We first felt the authentic Pain of our grief, but then felt new feelings of Joy from the visitation by Allen's spirit, which helped us step into new territory. As these Opposites met, and merged, something extraordinary had happened: the Wheel of Change moved and began a cosmic progression, and a healing occurred. In fact, we were bonused. *In an ephemeral fashion, the iridescent blue wings of the dragonfly took some of our grief and energetically EXCHANGED it for a lighter way of seeing things. Talk about the healing power of Opposites!*

Secret Number 10:
Others will help you See into the Miraculous.

As the hearts of Jim and I were softened, I immediately felt thankful he was there to help me see. During grief, when we feel most alone, there is more here to help us than we ever imagined, if only we turn our eyes to see it, and appreciate it.

When we are caught in the trenches of grief, Spirit puts others in our path. They can be people or dragonflies, or anything else Spirit decides to use to get our attention. They can be from this side, or the Other Side of the Veil (once again, the Yin Yang of Opposites informs us). In this case, Jim was there, and because he vocalized what was happening, we were able to share a magical moment together. He was also there when I heard of Allen's passing over. Plus, the energy of Spirit was there, alerting me through the blaring sirens of ambulances and a firetruck. And then the Spirit of the Dragonfly almost immediately helped both Jim and myself. When I think of it, many things were helping me (and us) to see into the Miraculous already! But as anyone knows who has gone through this, you also start getting Confirmations - ones that continually surprise you, if you but notice them.

These Confirmations and Signs of your Loved One's presence and continued care for you from the Other Side come in different ways. Within the week after Allen's passing over, my close friend had something to tell me. At first, she asked me, "What does Allen's signature look like? Does he sign his first name with an open A?"

The obvious answer was Yes. I showed her his signature on one of his Western photo prints. She blinked her eyes, took a breath, and relaxed enough to start telling me what had happened. As she did, I soon realized she'd asked about Allen's signature as her own way of Confirmation. She then proceeded to tell me how she got up at 2 A.M. to take care of her dog. As she sat in the rocking chair in the middle of her dining room, she saw Allen in his blue Schwan's uniform, clear as day!

Then she felt Allen's hand upon her shoulder.

"Please take care of Sheila," he said. *"Take care of Sheila."*

Now I hadn't seen this incredible vision of Allen, but my friend had! When I was most confused and dazed, his loving spirit had found a way to communicate to me. He simply visited my friend. And, so kindly, he also asked her to help me.

During these initial months, Allen would visit my friend not just once, but numerous times, always with the same enduring request. She answered his request and helped me very much. It helped Pain and Joy sit side by side. It cast Light into the Chaos of change.

Also, my other son, (step-son), Julian told me how he was surprised by something, too. He had learned that on his way "out of town" after his passing, Allen had stopped by and shook a special friend's hand in a dream. How beautiful.

Our Loved One has many ways of communicating with us, and all of them captured our attention. We could have ignored them, but they were not only heart-stopping, they were adding up. The fact that Higher Spirit was using such a variety of ways (and people) to get the message across made a big difference. Step by step, one magical event after another, we were learning to *Receive a new Lightness of Love. We tried to open our arms to messages from Allen and from Spirit, so we began listening and noticing, and eventually communicating in a New Way.*

The messages began tumbling through our lives, and were woven together, in Dreamtime and in real time, in remarkable ways.

Before we knew it, the time came for Allen's Celebration of Life. Because so many people were coming from the greater community, we had to find a larger space. We found a warm, spacious church, and as we visited, they asked us to take a tour of it so we'd know where everything was - including the restrooms. Nature called when I got to the women's restroom, so I took advantage of its presence.

As I came out of the stall, I noticed the unusual and very beautiful wallpaper. It went up an entire wall - a tall wall that lifted my eyes up, and up! My gosh, I had never seen such a wallpaper.

It was filled, simply filled, with - you guessed it - dragonflies!

My eyes went up and down, again and again, as I scratched my head in disbelief. And I left with a big smile. "You won't believe what I saw in the bathroom! Come in and see for yourself!"

We all trooped in and admired what we considered to be a masterpiece.

Later, as I spoke at Allen's Celebration of Life, I mentioned it, and asked how many ladies had ever seen a woman's bathroom decorated in dragonflies? Not one of them ever had!

But even more fascinating things happened at Allen's Celebration of Life, and the days leading up to it. Again, there were wings.

Chapter Five

Helpers:
The Eagle & the Hawk

I'd been thinking about this chapter for a while, of course, but immediately after I typed the words of the title, I looked up at the Oregon Public Broadcasting TV show I was listening to in the background. It featured one of my favorite singers, John Denver, and just a moment *after* I typed my title, another song came on. I lifted my head, and had to laugh. John began singing a song I love. I watched, suddenly transfixed, as even the title of his song appeared on the screen. Yep! "The Eagle and the Hawk."

I shook my head in amazement!

This synchronistic event, which happened today, definitely reflected the experiences I've been having for a decade, and even as recently as this week. It had begun with a dragonfly and now continued with an eagle.

Within the first weeks of Allen's passing, I went out on an errand. I liked the country road that connected two city areas. It was full of rolling meadows and tall fir trees. As I drove, my thoughts turned to Allen. Just as I was thinking how Allen loved the outdoors, like I did, something caught my eye. Off to my right, I glimpsed some bird wings - some pretty big bird wings - and then the unmistakable white head. Sure enough, it was a Bald Eagle! As I passed by in my car, I felt as if it was all happening in slow motion. The Bald Eagle's wings seemed to unfurl and flap in the same slow motion, as if matching me. It might have been a youngish Bald Eagle, as its wing expanse was not as great as some, but within the patient, confident movement of its wings, existed a power that made my heart stop as I took it in.

Sometimes there is a moment of time - a moment of inspiration - and you can't stop thinking about it. The powerful moment felt connected to Allen, yet I knew not how. So it was, that later on, when I opened a condolence card from my brother, I did a double-take: on the card a beautiful white-headed Bald Eagle soared through the Hoop of Life, and unfurled its broad wings into a cosmos of brilliant stars.

It was as if I was seeing the Bald Eagle from the country road all over again.

I read the kind card, with hand-written words that said, amongst other things: "Love is stronger than death. Allen now experiences God's LOVE."

Then I felt impelled to flip it over, and read the words printed on the back. I held my breath, and then felt a deep sigh escape from within me. It read simply:

Eagle's Flight

The Thunderbird in Native American
mythology will take a departed soul to
the next world. And thus a symbol of rebirth.

I still have this inspiring card. What a wonderful card for someone to choose, especially since they hadn't known about my sighting of this powerful Bald Eagle. My family is also part Native American (Cherokee), so I had an affinity for the artful way the symbolic card was designed. I was grateful this spirit bird had visited me on the country road near my home. We live in a world of untold mystery, and I was getting used to it on a broader scale than before.

That last summer, Allen was always seeing Red-Tailed Hawks soaring high above the trees. "Did you see that one?" he'd ask me. There was such excitement in his voice. But almost always my answer was a mystified, "No. Show me where it is."

With that given history, I was also surprised to start seeing Red-Tailed Hawks immediately after Allen's passing over. It became so frequent, I started laughing about it, and I found their appearances in my life to be more than mere sightings. Like the appearance of the dragonfly, the Red-Tailed Hawk's visits made me feel the strength of Allen's presence from beyond the Veil. I started noticing they almost always occurred when I needed comfort of some kind. How our Loved Ones respond to our needs and make this happen is quite remarkable to me, but when it happened in the first intense weeks after Allen's passing, it was especially appreciated.

As we prepared for Allen's Celebration of Life, it was a very hectic time. Much fell on my shoulders, and I didn't know if I could do it all. The night before, I had the first visitation from Allen in a dream. It was short and sweet. He came to tell me, "Yes, honey, you can get the house clean." That was it! The ceremony was the next day and afterward we would have lots of people in our home. At least half of Hillsboro was coming.

What kind of dream was this, I thought! After all, my friend was actually seeing Allen's spirit when he visited her at 2 A.M., and here I was, just getting a message about being able to clean the house! Well, we have to keep our sense of humor. That message was the very message I needed to hear, so the next morning I corralled my sons and we set to it. I was still very happy Allen had visited me in a dream.

Also, it's important to note how, when we are in the thicket of grief, we may not be able to have these kind of dreams, much less really coherent thoughts. Even if we feel peaceful, other emotions are tumbling through us, so much so that cleaning the house may feel like climbing a mountain. Many, many dreams would come later, but I am grateful Allen appeared to my friend so early on. That knowledge helped me through the ups and downs of my days and nights.

I think I made it through the next day's Celebration of Life because I felt the gift of so many Wings around me - from the hawk and eagle wings, to such ephemeral things as Allen's appearance in a dream. It helped me enter the day with a lighter spirit. As I faced the intensity of this loving celebration, the two men who helped me the most were my brave sons, who the night before faced their own grief and inability to do things, yet wrote and then read their personal eulogies to their beloved Dad. Even though they wrote them separately, I think it says something that they both called Allen "super-human." The following are their words, even the titles. The huge church was full to overflowing, but you could hear a pin drop as they spoke. Besides family and friends, the corporate team from Schwan's flew out from Minnesota. Afterward, the boys put on the song, "Simple Man" (which Julian alludes to in his eulogy) by Lynyrd Skynyrd. It was a favorite of Allen's, and both our sons liked it immensely. It spoke to them of their dad, such a good father and husband, who liked to work on our behalf, and love us so throughly. While it played, they lit candles in Allen's honor.

Julian's Tribute to Dad

It is overwhelming to see the turnout gathered here today. Obviously, our father's love, optimism and generosity has touched many of you. My dad had an enormous heart. You all knew him as the Schwan's man with character. I knew him as a man that was always there for me, he always had kind words, advice, and a solution to every situation I threw at him. My dad was super-human.

It is unfortunate to have him taken from us at the young age of 57 - but I am comforted by the fact that there was a circle of love and trust. Some families and friends don't have the chance to experience that bond. It was hard for me not to focus on the negative about this situation. I know that my dad would tell me to suck it up, and look for the positive. He was such a winner. I am also grateful to have had such an amazing man for a father. It is because of Allen Stephens that I turned out so well (laugh).

My dad was a simple man. When I was growing up he would constantly eat tuna and white rice. I would ask him why, and he would tell me about his experiences in Japan. You could ask him about anything and he would have something interesting to say. A true storyteller he was. Most of them were true too. My dad would also spout off jokes that weren't always funny, but just the fact that he was trying to make us laugh warmed our hearts. I will miss that. I will miss driving at night with him, his obsession with the Blazers, stacking firewood, watching TV together, his smile, doing laundry together, telling him secrets, camping, painting the house, playing basketball on the court we all built together, beef stroganoff, snowy days on Oak St., laughing together, wrestling, his hugs, water balloon fights with all the kids from the neighborhood coming over, our first bike rides, mowing the lawn together, shooting bb guns - there are so many memories that I can't even tell you.

The last time I talked to my dad was a week and a half ago. I told him that I was starting a new job and that I was stressed. He told me that I would rock that job and that he would pray for me. It brings tears to my eyes to think that was the last conversation we had. But when u think about it, we could not have parted on better terms. I wish I would have spent more time with him in the last few years, but I know he loved me, us, and all of you. I know for a fact that he felt all of our love.

I will miss him so much but I will carry him in my heart every day.

All of us laughed and cried as we heard Julian's heartfelt words. They mean the world to me and Jim.

These are Jim's words:

Jim's Prayer

Dear God, We love you, and as we love you, so too do we love my father, Allen, who you've just welcomed home to you. We know he sees our love for him with unveiled eyes now, and is finally aware of how profound a respect and admiration we held for him. God, when my dad was here with us, your spirit flowed thru me into him in the form of the care, love, and kindness that I gave to him, but teach me now, God, how to refocus my application of your love to others so that others may behold the beauty that you inspired within me which i shared with my father. Let everyone I touch, God, feel more potently your love as it is boosted by my father's return to your side.

God, I miss my dad, I miss him so much, and i know missing him is only natural, but i feel your hand, and my father's together steer me to touch those whom I long to touch that are still here: so I greet the new day with my love for you, God, and with my love for my father, Allen, flowing from me into those i meet.

So many times I told my dad he was a superhero, and now I know he sees how I was not kidding or trying to boost his ego, now he sees how truly superhuman he was to me.

Help me to allow my father to stand behind me, God, as you do; holding me upright when i am unable to stand. God, help me to add my father to the wellspring of good intention that flows into the world from me, help me let my father rest in peace, and help me to love others in the unconditional, patient, loving, sweet, steadfast, kind, and forgiving way that my father, Allen, showed me and taught me to perpetuate, for now I am a part of the legacy of my father's love; help me to do my father honor, God, so that he may smile down upon me until the day of my ascension to your side.

In your name, o King of Grace, I do pray,
Amen.

All of us sighed and cried as we took in Jim's love and peace. It inspired us to go on, by not letting go of Allen's love, but by letting it in.

It still helps me, to read these loving words from my sons. They both have such good hearts. I can feel their wonderful, loving father in each of them.

Then, as part of my eulogy, I read my wedding vows, written to Allen 23 years earlier. I had written them as a poem, and now I spoke it as though I was reading it all over again, to Allen. It was my gift to him that day.

"When Words Are Not Enough"

There comes a point
when love has conquered words,
and no longer can i say
and have it expressed
     in wholeness.

I will have to give you blueberries
          instead,
knowing your love for them.
I will have to paint your ceiling with stars
and point to each one, separately,
when wanting to give back to you
what has already been given.

I will have to make banners of silk
in the finest shades of sun
to meet you at the door.
I will have to take you on a ride
to eagle spirit's world when tiredness haunts you.
Together we will taste the heaven's touch;
know no fear;
meet our true selves
above the cast of clouds.

I will have to caress you
          many times,
bring rivers to your door,
sweep all worries into mellowness.

And then, as winter comes,
i will have to find all the flowers
that bloom when times are sparse,
when spirits feel so bare.

But you have taught me well;
          beyond words
there is something else.
And wholeness comes
in the layers of expansiveness,
in the quiet language of your Love.

At the end of our dear Allen's Celebration of Life, we opened up the microphone, so people could speak. One after another, their love for him spilled out. So many people spoke, that in a humorous way, we were a bit relieved when they finally stopped so we could all make it to our home for further sharing. Each of them said Allen was their best friend. And they all told us how Allen spoke endlessly and lovingly about me and the boys. I felt comforted by the broad shoulders of our two brave sons, just 26 and 27, who had stood like men that day, and made their father and me so proud.

One of our friends, Bev Martin, couldn't attend the entire ceremony, but came in half-way through, at the moment I was speaking. I looked up and drew great strength from her. I had put Allen's Western buckskin jacket around my shoulders, to lighten up the celebration, both for others and myself. I read the last chapter from the manuscript of Allen's Western novel, "Gone to Glory," and talked about the sentiments on the Bald Eagle card, and my Red-Tailed Hawk sightings. We'd asked Bev to give the service, but because of a workshop she was giving, her wonderful husband, Jim, had guided us through the ceremony, doing an exquisite job. So I was very surprised and glad to see my dear friend, Bev, standing in the back of the room, literally giving me back-up as I held back my tears in order to speak about Allen.

When Bev and I finally caught up with each other, she told me there was something she just had to share about her meditation workshop which she was in the middle of giving. She'd taken her break time to drive over, just so she could be with us. "It has been quite unusual really," she said, "when the workshop participants close their eyes to meditate, they all keep seeing hawks. Hawks, and more hawks - and no one has a clue as to why!"

She grinned broadly, "Now I know why!"

In addition to the knowledge of Allen's presence at his celebration, via the beautiful hawk appearances at the meditation workshop, I also now see something in my wedding vows - something I had never noticed before. I see the eagle in the verse; *"I will have to take you on a ride/to eagle spirit's world when tiredness haunts you./Together we will taste the heaven's touch."*

In so many ways, Allen was opening the doors to heaven's touch for me. And wings seemed to lead the way - first with dragonflies, and eagles, and now also with Red-Tailed Hawks.

The Celebration of Life was just that, a huge celebration. As we left, Julian pointed upward. *In the sky, was the sun, surrounded by a soft rainbow circle. This amazing, full circle was something we had never seen before.* Fortunately, Julian took a photo of it that we still hold dear.

The photo of the Rainbow Circle was an Event, after other momentous Events, that we could look back on years later, and feel how it was continuing to move our hearts. Just today, I found out this phenomenon is called "a halo." That fits, all right!

A week or so after the celebration for Allen, I went to visit Bev at her home, which, like mine, has a greenspace behind it. As we spoke, something caught Bev's eye. "Look," she said. Much as it was like when I was with Allen, I didn't see what she was pointing at.

"Look! It's a Red-Tailed Hawk!" Bev said.

I looked and looked but couldn't see it. But then, as if helping me, the hawk lifted its great expanse of wings, and flew out of the tall fir tree, into the sky - so I could see it.

Bev and I just looked at each other, and smiled as big, happy tears spilled from my eyes.

Many friends helped my sons and I to see in those first days. But as the Red-Tailed Hawks and the dragonflies kept coming to visit, we became very adept at understanding Allen's loving spirit was around us - and we thanked him.

More magical moments kept happening to us, and soon, as the Australian aborigine's teach us, these extraordinary experiences would weave a whole new world into existence. It is in this more expanded version of home that I now live.

This magical weaving by Spirit would come in artful, thought-provoking, and even comical ways. It would come through dragonflies, Red-Tailed Hawks, and even some very memorable dogs . . .

Chapter Six

Messages from Dragonflies,
Hawks & Shaggy Dogs

Alone at my kitchen table one morning, I hunted for ways I could thank everyone for all the kind sentiments, the beautiful cards, and for taking part in Allen's Celebration of Life.   After the ceremony, the boys and I stood for a what seemed forever, receiving hugs and thoughtful words from a long line of friends. Allen had friends from everywhere, but the ones from his Schwan's route in Hillsboro somehow figured out how half of them would come to the Celebration of Life, and half would come to our home afterward. Now, how could our family begin to thank them?

Since some of them had missed the Celebration at the church, I decided to include a copy of Julian's and Jim's eulogies, and my wedding vow poem in the thank you packet. And I decided to mention how the wings of the iridescent blue dragonfly had met us at the door the day after Allen's shocking passing.

As I thought about it, an interesting thing happened. I suddenly remembered another dragonfly visitation which I had totally forgotten about until now. As I've said, all summer and into the Indian Summer of fall, Allen and I had been seeing dragonflies on our back deck. This was the second summer in our new home, and we'd spent the whole summer working on planting trees, shrubs, and flowers. To top it off, I had asked my woodworking husband to "merely" build a deck, and then he also wanted to build a water feature to top off the look of the yard.

Allen liked these kinds of projects, and he happily got started. As soon as he began, I realized what a big project it was. Even though I'd imagined getting it done quickly, he proceeded with a loving craftsmanship I thoroughly admired. He went at the pace of love.

So it was that after everything was planted, and he'd completed our beautiful deck, we celebrated. Whew! This home was now ours to totally enjoy.

After Allen went to work the next morning, I went out on the deck to just live in the moment, and appreciate our work. It had paid off. As I took it all in - the blooming daisies and delphiniums, the green leaves moving gently in the birch tree, and the warm wood deck where we could entertain friends, I also realized that I could use this peaceful deck as my place to come and meditate and pray.

Ahhh, I stretched my arms out joyfully, and then I let them drift to my sides. As I offered up my first prayers, something whizzed by me. Then it was right in front of my face, just ten inches away - as if it was looking at me! It was a beautiful dragonfly, a friendly one at that. But as I admired it, something else happened - it landed, ever so lightly, on my right shoulder.

Oh my gosh, there's a dragonfly on my shoulder! I'd never had such a thing happen to me. Even though I felt like hopping up and down in excitement, I tried to keep still. Amazingly, the dragonfly was happy on my shoulder and didn't move, so then I looked at it. "Well, aren't you beautiful," I said. And it stayed there, perched on my shoulder even as I talked and turned my head to see it better. It was exquisite!

After what seemed like a long time, the dragonfly took flight.

I realized I had experienced a miraculous moment as time stopped, and it was only me and the dragonfly.

Now, as I sat at my dining room window, thinking about thank you notes, I remembered all this, and how it paralleled the new dragonfly visitation on the day after Allen's passing. Wow, this is remarkable, I thought.

Then it dawned on me that I also had been impelled to write a poem about it! How could I not have thought about all this before now! I guess it was the fog of grief. It's a strange thing.

The poem I had written was unlike most of my poems, in which I receive some kind of insight at the end. But this one, while it celebrated the dragonfly, was open-ended. After I finished writing the poem, I knew only that the dragonfly was a harbinger - a harbinger of some mystery I was yet to understand. This was a very unusual poem for me to write, as my poems are a way for me to commune, and they open the doors for understandings from Spirit. Many ah-ha's have reached my fingertips this way.

"Upon My Shoulder"

Such a work of art, building the garden is.
First the vision.
What will be.
What will fill the space
and turn dirt and weeds
into the softness we all need.

Next, the work.
The shovel bent into the task,
the sweat that beads the brow,
then cascades down
into some new kind of waterfall!

I laugh at all I've done
to get this far,
to have a garden
where once was none.

But this morning
a new thought competes
for the need to plant
or seed or weed,
and says a truth
I'd yearned to hear -
that my garden is not complete
until I stop the garden's
work and toil,
and go there
just to let God in.

So willingly, I step into a garden

that wants to tend to me -
and within a heartbeat
I have a partner on the restful glider,
always sitting with me, encouraging me,
and as I slip into the mystery,
I stretch out my legs
and swing free.

Before I leave, I stand and bow my head
to check out the tadpoles
that had appeared unexpectedly
in the pond of water lilies.

In a second, I realize
I'm taking time for things.
That I'm somehow in sync.
And in that split second
a Dragonfly buzzes into
view, then pauses,
like a helicopter in mid-flight -
and decides to land.

I must be in my garden again,
for the brilliant blue, shimmering Wings
land upon my shoulder,
and act as if they never want to leave . . .

As I shared about the dragonfly in my thank you note, I couldn't believe all the interwoven threads that came into play, each at their perfect time. I was struck once again by this magical event, because the dragonfly that had come to visit me in the garden - my new place to pray - and had lingered so confidently on my shoulder, also had beautiful wings. In fact, it had *iridescent blue wings!* - just like the dragonfly that visited us at our front door the first day after Allen's passing!

I saw then how the visit from the dragonfly had been a harbinger - of Allen's upcoming death. No wonder that was left as a mystery for me until after Allen's passing. Now it stood as a Sacred Preparation. An artful act of Sacred Preparation, where in, when looking back, my heart could be comforted at how a spiritual path of destiny was unfolding.

Secret Number 11:
*Sacred Preparations
and Confirmations
will help you understand
the Design of your Life.*

If you but notice, you will receive Confirmations, both in the present, and from your past. The ones woven into your past are confirmations of Sacred Preparations, designed to bring you peace and light your path.

The beauty of these moments - both the visitation from the dragonfly, and the fact that I didn't remember it until after Allen's passing - left me in awe. And then, when I also realized I'd written the poem about it, much less the evocative, harbinger-of-things-yet-to-come feeling - well, it all added up to a beautiful weaving. Spirit's touch was throughout it all, both before and after Allen passed over.

It suggested Allen's death was not "an accident" - that it was somehow part of his destiny, the Divine Plan of his life. If that was the case, then it was also part of mine. *It was then I really started concentrating not on "why" this had happened to me, but on "what I was to learn" in all of this.*

Besides these signs of artful Preparation, some of the signs of Sacred Preparation were a bit more comical, but equally significant. After Allen's Celebration of Life, Julian, Jim and myself went to a place where I grew up, on Salmon River near Mt. Hood. This is where we had also taken the ashes of Allen's mother, Evelyn, years earlier. We stood on what we call "The Big Rock," and as we thought of her and said our prayers, a Monarch butterfly flew around us, wisping between us, and definitely getting our attention. Eventually all of us shook our heads in acknowledgement of this beautiful touch of "angel wings" from Allen's mom. Now I wondered if the butterfly would be back today, as we spread Allen's ashes into the sparkling river, but alas, it was not.

It was still a beautiful moment when just the three of us talked about our special dad and husband. We'd wanted this moment alone, as a family. The only thing interrupting our outdoor ceremony was a big old dog - like a big sheep dog whose floppy hair almost covered his eyes. Its size was a bit intimidating to me, as I'd been bitten by a couple dogs when I was younger, and it was quickly making its way straight to us. I scooted behind my son, Jim, for a little safety if needed. I didn't feel at all comfortable and we couldn't tell where the big dog had come from, as its owners weren't anywhere in sight. We really didn't want to stop our ceremony to deal with this dog or pay attention to it, but the dog persisted, artfully making his way around Jim, determined it seemed, to softly poke his head into my leg like he knew me, and was glad to be part of the group.

So I talked to it. "Hi fella. Aren't you a beautiful one." I petted him, and he used his body weight to stand his ground, but in a very loving and happy way. As the gentle giant refused our equally gentle commands for him to go home, it dawned on me that he was here to stay. He seemed to want to be right in the middle of our ceremony - so as his tail continued to peacefully wag, we allowed him in until something struck me. I said, half-laughingly, then quite seriously, to the boys, "Maybe this is Allen visiting us!"

As I bent down to pet him again, I said, "Thank you, Allen." He responded, of course, by immediately wagging his tail more vigorously. Then he showed his affectionate nature by quickly licking me in the face! It was a good thing for him that he did it quickly, because if I'd known it was coming, I would probably have avoided it!

That night, during my quiet time, I lifted my thoughts to Allen's. "Was that you today at the Big Rock? And if so, why did you come as a dog???"

"That was the only way I could kiss you!" came the surprising reply.

As any woman would say, that was a very good line. Even if it was about a dog! Not only was Allen good at making us laugh by telling jokes when he was alive, but now it seemed he was *still* making me laugh.

This blends into another moment with Allen - a more serious series of moments. It was the weekend before Allen's death, and Jim, Allen and I were all down with the flu. We were taking care of each other, and giving each other some love, but that was about it.

When I went into the kitchen, Allen followed me, and told me how there was this really mean dog on his Schwan's route. His customer warned him not to pet the dog, under any circumstances, and he had stayed clear, until this week.

Now Allen loved dogs and cats so much, his customers called him the Dog Whisperer. Once Allen had been warned about a cat. "Don't pet it - it will claw you!" His customer left the room and when she came back, the "terrible cat" was luxuriously lounging on Allen's shoulders, ready to take a nap!

"I decided to pet that dog," Allen continued. "It was the only one I hadn't been able to make friends with."

"And then what happened?" I queried, surprised at his actions.

"The dog turned over, showed me his belly, and let me pet him to my heart's content."

When your husband has a route with lots of dogs on it, you want him to avoid being bitten, and all the damage it can accidentally do to his hand or arm. Allen carried his own dog biscuits for them, in fact he bought them himself, but that was no assurance a mean dog wouldn't bite him. I was happy for Allen, and amazed, but I was still concerned.

"So just why in the world would you pet a mean dog?" I asked.

"Because I didn't want to die afraid of a dog."

The answer itself surprised me, yet I didn't take it seriously. Then Allen continued the conversation, going into territory I had broached before, but one he had never directly brought up. He talked about what I would do if and when he passed over. This is a subject many couples talk about, of course, but as I said, it was a first for Allen.

I told Allen how, even though I would feel like following him, just as the Native Americans may have gone out and sat under a tree and waited for death to take them after their spouse had died, I could not do that. Jim was sick and needed me. He would need me for a long time.

We looked into each other's eyes, and hugged for a long time.

The love between Allen and myself was very strong. We were so close, that saying I couldn't follow him when the time came was a huge, very difficult statement for me.

Of course we were sick with the flu that weekend, and talking in 'what if's', but the conversation hit me hard. Two days later, Allen was killed. You never know how long you have with your loved one, but on the Monday before his death, after I had kissed and hugged Allen goodbye as he left for work, I felt the urge to follow him out onto the path by our front door, and I gave him another big hug and kiss.

"I love you, honey."

"I really love you too, sweetheart."

I was so glad I followed him out for what would become our very last moment together. I was glad I made it a good one.

During these months before his passing, Allen was as happy as he'd ever been. A wonderful intuitive, and now good friend, Candia Sanders, explained what Spirit told her was happening. In the time before Allen's passing, his body was showing signs of weakness. He had to go on a new medicine, and he also had to stop eating all wheat products. But this was a sign of Allen's destiny. He and I had worked so much out over the years, and had come to such a high level of love, that his assignment was complete. Consciously, though, he didn't understand this, and was frustrated by his body's new frailties. He wanted to work through anything and everything, so he could stay with me and our boys.

But subconsciously, part of him knew, and his internal self was somehow dealing with it, even if he didn't understand it consciously. Spirit has a way of getting us ready, even though our own spirit may be trying to renegotiate the contract.

I like the way Betty Eadie expresses it in her popular book, "Embraced by the Light." My own version goes something like this: Before we are born, we sit at the hand of God. We converse about what our challenges will be. Because we are filled with and surrounded by such brilliant Unconditional Love, we are ambitious. We want plenty of challenges, because they will polish our soul. But God wisely asks if that isn't a bit much, and suggests we pare them down a bit. The time (or a few potential times) of our passing over is also decided. And it also takes into consideration the opportunity for growth this will provide to the people around you, like your loved ones.

Even these Sacred Preparations - or these ways that let you know it was your loved one's time to pass over - will be woven into your life tapestry.

So this is why I cherish the dragonfly's visit on my deck before Allen died, and then the story of why he didn't want to die afraid of a dog. Or why I felt impelled to give Allen an extra hug. They seem to be Spirit's indicators, or Spirit's heads-up that this is part of the plan.

Amazingly, when the potentially mean dog pushed his way into our circle at the Big Rock by Salmon River, I found I wasn't afraid of a dog either. And I guess I wasn't the only one who wanted to give an extra kiss! These moments help to lighten the load, and make us wonder or laugh, as we bravely go forward. We don't consciously know everything that is in our agreements with our Creator, but I've found part of my agreement is to live with Allen in my heart, and see the loving purposes I've yet to fulfill.

Even Pennies from Heaven have been part of the path that keeps leading me forward, into the mysteries of living with help from the Other Side of the Veil.

Chapter Seven

Pennies from Heaven,
& the Birth-Day

As I look back on my path of healing during grief, I notice how many friends were part of that healing. The way they helped me began to pierce the armor of my pain as I struggled to find my way. Each event surrounding all this help had a little mystery to it. Some were seemingly simple events, and some were more complex, but they all had some mystery around them - the good kind of mystery. Somehow the distinctness of these events helped them remain in my heart as touchstones, reminding me to think big when it comes to Higher Spirit's ways of giving us messages.

One of my friends, Kay Allenbaugh, is the best-selling author of the "Chocolate for a Woman's Soul" book series. My stories and poems were part of many of these books, but I was also able to be part of the bond Kay created within this fine group. I remember reading Kay's story, "The Sweat Lodge" in her first book, "Chocolate for a Woman's Soul." I knew then that I wanted to be part of whatever she was doing because the story was about her mom, who had died when Kay was young. Kay went through her life without her mom by her side. Then she went to a sweat lodge, and came out thinking absolutely nothing had happened. No insight. Just nothing! In fact, she was so exhausted, she collapsed, outstretched upon the sand - only to experience her mother's face in the moon. Her mother talked to Kay in words only she could understand - showing Kay how, all along, she had been there with her, at all the pivotal moments of her life, and then some!

Kay came into my life while Allen was still alive, and as she and I shared tea and talked one day, I received an insight for her. Recently her dad had died, and she was wondering about him. To my surprise, I received a vision of him sending her Pennies. I said, "Kay, what in the world is this? I mean, it is so common. Why pennies?" I was bewildered.   But as I talked, Kay slowly began smiling, telling me how she'd been seeing all kinds of pennies lately, in unusual ways, like they were just dropped in front of her.

"Oh my goodness," Kay's eyes lit up while she talked. "These are Pennies from Heaven!" Never having heard the term, I asked her to explain. So I found out how many people, who have faced the loss of someone they love, have had these hard-to-miss experiences with pennies afterward - so many people, in fact, they "coined" a term for it!

The fact I had this vision of her dad sending her these "Pennies from Heaven" when I didn't know anything about the mystical nature of the event, was enlightening and comforting to both of us. It helped Kay with her relationship with her dad, and it opened up my eyes to something people experience that I'd never heard of before then. The way her dad had given her a Penny from Heaven, by giving me a vision about it, was very creative of him!

Because of my experience with Kay, I paid attention when I eventually started seeing pennies in these unusual kinds of ways, but I was not convinced it was more than mere coincidence. Grief can be stubborn. I also like very clear signs. So I had told Jim about it, but that was just about the extent of it.

Maybe that's why it surprised both Jim and myself so much. Here we were, one ordinary day, at a Border's Bookstore. As we tried to make the most of standing in the long check-out line, a bright penny fell right at our feet. We both looked around, but it hadn't come from anyone. For some reason, we both looked up immediately, and spotted an unusual puff of dust rising directly from an open rafter maybe 30 feet above our heads. There was nothing else around that it could have fallen from, and there was no way for someone to get up on the high ceiling rafter, much less near it.

We looked back and forth at each other, and again and again at the small cloud of dust above the rafter, directly in line with the penny. It was really high, and we still could find no reason for the small cloud of dust to even be there!

"Pennies from Heaven" will get you like that. It happens in the middle of your ordinary day. But it's different. As you pick the penny up, it gets to you. You put it safely in your pocket and keep it for a while, maybe for a long time or a short time. And you know. Something quiet and loving moves past the armor around your grieving heart, and happily settles in to stay. Even if just your son and you know, you don't care; you aren't concerned if other people get it or not. The small but mysterious event is yours to keep, and when you touch it in your pocket, or place it on a shelf where you can see it often, you know the kind of things Kay learned after the sweat lodge.

You know your Loved One is with you.

As I think back to the last bright penny that caught my attention, the one I mentioned that flashed and caught my eye in my car when I first began writing this book, I see not a mere coincidence, but a creative expression of a devoted kind of Love.

These "Pennies from Heaven" are sometimes actual pennies, and sometimes they are other things. They are gifts and signs from the Other Side, and they come in all kinds of mysterious but very real ways. And they help you when you need it most.

After the uplifting energy from Allen's Celebration of Life was over, the ups and downs of reality set in, and I missed his daily physical presence in my life. The sadness I felt about Allen's departing became heavy on my heart. As I was feeling particularly down and confused one day, Allen's good friend from Hillsboro called me. As I talked to her, my feelings poured out unexpectedly. "Is it real?" I wondered. "Are these moments of grace I'm experiencing real?" Even over the phone, I wept.

Fortunately, our friend, E.T. was the perfect person to talk to, as she'd lost her dad, and had many experiences that showed her his presence in her life, even to this day. In the middle of my painful fog, it was incredible to hear all the moments when her dad's spirit had connected with her, and had shown her the strength and endurance of his Love.

Now E.T. was paying it forward, showing by example, that I wasn't crazy, that these moments of connection are real, and that they can continue over the span of time, if you let them. It is amazing how E.T. called at just the moment I needed to hear what she had to say. But even as we were talking, I knew it wasn't just a coincidence.

It brought me back to a place of Peace. And I began to settle in to a new season of my grieving. I still had to practice remembering these graceful, synchronistic events which were cracking my heart open, but I felt different. Like I had a launching pad.

One day I was alone, but it was in a good way. All the demanding hubbub of life insurance, funeral preparations, endless paperwork, and the planning for Allen's Celebration of Life was over, and I found myself relaxing in my living room. I remember exactly where it was when it happened. It was like some beautiful essence just came in and suspended time. Much like my friend who had seen a vision of Allen when she was just sitting in a chair at 2 A.M., I found myself sitting in a chair when it happened, too, but for me it was about 2 P.M. in the afternoon.

I saw and felt a vision, an incredible vision unlike any I had ever known. My heart expanded into the light of it, as right in front of me, I saw and felt the energetic vision of Allen's spirit at the actual moments when he passed over. I had seen and felt some images before, in the first moments I had learned about his death, but this time I was shown even more detail. Like it was the uncut version. And as I saw it, I felt a deep Peace flow into my whole being and beyond, filling the living room with a feeling of Light and great Loving joy.

It started with the glow of his spirit, and then showed his spirit as an incredible, glowing golden Light that literally sparkled as it ascended. As it lifted, this Light became a beautiful Spiral that makes you want to smile a million smiles as you feel it.

It took its time to ascend, as if wanting to show me the experience. The golden spiral was so beautiful! It was Allen, as his spirit met and merged with the enormous Love from Spirit. He was not only surrounded by the beaming sun of massive Unconditional Love; he became part of the Love!

The spiral of his spirit uniting with Spirit moved upward like the most graceful dancer. Then it burst through to the Other Side, and everyone cheered. Fireworks exploded in joy.

At that moment, I was given an awesome understanding:

Why the fireworks?

Because it was Allen's BIRTH-DAY!, I was told.

He had come home - and it was his Birth-Day, of course!

Oh my gosh! It makes all the sense in the world now, but I had never thought about it that way before.

As the fireworks continued, I was shown how Allen's spirit was already multidimensional. Now in energy form, Allen's spirit was also in the magnificent fireworks as they burst forth, showering Love everywhere. His spirit was still able to stay on the Other Side, but his transformed spirit also burst forth into this life, and his Love became a part of everything. It showered into the plants and other things, and it showered into the hearts of people, blessing them. The Higher Love his advanced spirit was now bringing from the Other Side was a gift of incredible proportions, so when we care for other people, here on earth, we are also appreciating the Loving energy from the Other Side - and we can work in tandem with this multifaceted Love by nurturing it.

There is much healing to be done, and now I saw there was even more Love at our fingertips. It gives me a lot to think about.

The beautiful energy of Allen's love also showed me some other things, and gave me some personal guidance, which I very much appreciated.

I sighed, and kept this vision of the beautiful Ascension of Allen's spirit to myself at first. After all, it was mind-blowing to me. So unexpected. Then I couldn't keep the beauty of it inside me any longer, so I told two close girlfriends, but not even my boys.

Three months later, Jim had a dream, a dream in which Allen's spirit was a golden spiral that became fireworks when he passed over, and then Allen's loving energy was sprinkled into the everything, and into people. And then Jim received exactly the same personal guidance for me that I had received!

Sometimes you are speechless. You try to talk, but you stutter.

Finally I was able to get the words out, and share my own vision with Jim. I don't know why I hadn't before, but it seemed guided that I had not done so. Now, as we shared notes, we had confirmation of a vision that had visited both of us. E.T. was right.

This great stuff happens, and it explodes like 4th of July fireworks in our hearts.

It was, and is, the most beautiful vision I have ever received. It informs the way I look at everything.

I also think it is no coincidence that Jim is my son. He is a sensitive soul who sees deeply into life, and makes me feel more comfortable as I follow the same path of living beyond the surface of things. I often remark that life is not just a shopping trip, and Jim laughs in agreement. It's nice to have a pal.

But one day during the first Christmas holiday without Allen, I went out alone, without my helpful sidekick. As I set out in my silver Buick to do a very real thing - ironically, to shop - not in the superficial-shopping-trip-of-life way, but to shop for meaningful presents that might lift both my sons' spirits as we faced a new difficulty. Our Christmas times as a family had been so happy, so heartwarming and fun.

Now what would they be like? What could I do, as a mom, to help us?

It wasn't easy to get into my car, much less point it in the right direction, and try to do all this alone. Allen and I had always shared most of the Christmas shopping. I didn't want to go through all these different things alone. But it had to be done. Emotions surged through me like a rain cloud. "I don't know if I can do this," I thought to myself as I passed through the major intersection in our town. "This is harder than I'd imagined!"

And all at once, there it was . . .

It lifted off a sign post on the right side of the road with one powerful stroke, and flew so close to my Buick that I gasped.

Across my windshield, from right to left, flew a magnificent hawk - a Red-Tailed Hawk!

As I gasped, I wiped away my tears.

This is an "event."

This doesn't just happen.

This has never happened to me before!

I proceeded on my shopping trip, feeling the presence of Allen's spirit through the broad, strong wings of a master flyer.

During Christmas, New Year's, and the coming year, I knew I was not alone.

The boys, of course, knew about this. Years later, we were talking about it as Jim and I went Christmas shopping together, this time in my new cranberry Buick LaCrosse. It was helpful to have him with me. The pain of grief never goes away; but it softens. As Raymond Moody, M.D., says, the hole in your heart gets smaller. And being with people you love helps immensely, so I was feeling comforted by his presence beside me. It was raining hard, and I was paying attention to the roads and the holiday traffic. As we grew near the same intersection, I noticed something in my peripheral vision. It was suddenly near me, and to my left.

"Jim," I sputtered . . .

And then I made out what it was. Here it was - again - the Red-Tailed Hawk! This was the closest a hawk had ever been! We both watched in utter amazement as it unfurled its majestic wings in front of our windshield in the storm. It was heart-stopping. Not more than 4 inches above the front hood of my car, it flew "with us" as if slowing down time. Each beat of its wings came so close, I thought we might hit it. But the majestic bird had it under control as it flew forward diagonally to the right side - Jim's side - of the car, as if to say, "I'm visiting you, too, Jim."

It was so close though, I kept my foot above the brake, just in case! Both Jim and I watched intently as each moment unfolded. Caught in a what felt like a beautiful dream-like state, I held my breath. As time settled into a hush, everything else fell away. *The great hawk was so close to us, we even saw long pieces of grass in its talon!*

The power and up-close details of it drifted across our vision, creating an indelible impression. We knew this was something we never wanted to forget.

The dramatic slow-motion picture seemed to stay like that forever. I felt like saying, "How is it doing that?"

And then, as if by magic, the remarkable bird was gone, into the storm. The rain pelted down on us, and I was glad I hadn't hit another vehicle.

Jim and I just looked at each other.

"Mom," he said, *"That was a miracle!"*

So it was that I was no longer the only carrier of the miracle. As with the vision of Allen's 4th of July type of Birth-Day celebration, now Jim and I carried the knowledge of the miracles - together.

And I was glad.

Jim came over to my house on another important occasion, to honor the day that Allen had passed over. It was a year or so later, but Jim knows the day can still be hard on me, and he wants to be there to soften the load. We talked and shared some of our good memories of Allen, a simple thing really. Nothing special had to be done on this day. Talking about Allen was special enough. It met the needs of our hearts.

We opened the garage door and chatted. I wasn't in a hurry to see Jim go. The fresh October air felt good.

As we walked outside, Jim paused and gently said he felt Allen near us. Sometimes Jim could feel or see things I did not, and the fact he felt Allen's energy near us was a big gift to me. Then Jim turned toward his car, and gazed down the street.

"Mom," he said, "Look at that!"

"What?" I said, a little oblivious.

"Look at the sky!"

As I followed his line of vision, I saw it. On this somewhat misty day, a rainbow radiated across the our line of sight, right in our neighborhood. It arched its soft colors across the sky.

"Look real close, Mom," Jim continued.

As I did, I saw not one rainbow, but two. A beautiful Double Rainbow emerged from the grey cloudy sky.

And as we looked yet another emerged. It was faint, but still there. *In the light, it would fade in and out, as if showing us the presence of the invisible world, which was unseen, but just beyond our sight.*

Jim and I instantly thought back to the time of Allen's Celebration of Life, which I've mentioned - when we stepped out of church and Julian pointed out the Rainbow Circle around the sun.

Jim put his arm around me and together we gazed at the rainbows. "Well Dad," he said softly but confidently, "We get it. We really appreciate that you are here for us." He squeezed my arm. "Always here."

Secret Number 12:
Double Confirmations are Double Miracles -
Spirit sends People and Events
meant to Awaken our Higher Vision

When I finished writing this, I relaxed and watched a movie, "The Color of Rain," on the Hallmark Channel. It was about the grieving of a spouse. The woman wanted a sign, and while taking a hike on a camping trip, her companion smiled and said, "There it is."

She looked up and there was her sign, bright as day. She saw a rainbow - a stunning Double Rainbow at that. When it came up on the TV screen, it was just like it came up into view outside my front yard that day with my son, Jim.

In this way, Spirit seems to be saying, "Yes, this is a chapter about confirmations, even double confirmations" - for after I read Jim's words, "Always here," I remembered Allen's Western novel. They were the last two words of his final chapter!

And, to underline everything, Spirit must have had a hand in the third, somewhat funny confirmation. Again on the TV screen, when it was on pause, a meaningful tidbit appeared. It said: *Neanderthals made jewelry out of hawks' talons.*

I mean, you can't make this stuff up. I thought not to include this third confirmation, but Spirit has a reason for everything. I talked with a great waitress, Sheena, at one of my favorite local restaurants yesterday. She'd lost her mother about a year ago, and her mom's spirit had visited her as a beautiful butterfly more than once, but it was still hitting her hard. She'd had confirmations, but she needed more. We all do.

I have learned to follow Spirit's guidance, even if it embarrasses me a bit. But indeed, the quote about the hawks' talons - and about the Neanderthals - is a corker. And Spirit does love to see us laugh.

Because of these mother-son moments of cosmic partnership, maybe it's not so surprising that on Valentine's Day, when Jim and I were leaving the Home Depot store, Jim saw another beautiful hawk perched on the top of a light pole. "Look at that!" Jim said (again!). As I followed his finger, I saw it clearly. I love it when they are sitting there; the hawks have such clout. They own the space.

"Let's get closer," Jim said.

The adventure was on!

We must have looked pretty funny to someone else as we drove ever so slowly, closer and closer to the light pole at the empty outer limits of the parking lot. It is amazing what other people don't see. But then again, I was helped by Jim. We were both really thrilled when the Red-Tailed Hawk stayed put, peacefully holding its ground, even when we were just 15 feet away - as if to say, "Come over for a visit."

That was quite a treat for this widow, quite a sight for sore eyes on Valentine's Day!

These many moments of grace were adding up to form quite a collection now, and both Jim and I took notice. It was like we were in on the game - the very real game of being blessed by our Loved One's healing presence in our lives. We realized this was a craft - this noticing and honoring of the sacred messages of comfort coming on the wings of Love in so many ways. Many caring people were placed in these sacred moments, when Allen's spirit stepped in to say, "Hello. I am *always with you.*"

I consider these gifts from the Other Side, all so varied and all so beautiful, to be my special "Pennies from Heaven." They are the riches that tenderly - and boldly - helped me with my own type of ascension, back into my real life that now held whole new dimensions. Amazingly, they didn't make me want to live in the past. I became curious about these beautiful gifts, and how they could affect my future life - for the better.

Chapter Eight

*The Grief Group;
The Magic of
Finding My Voice*

"I learn by going where I have to go."
- Theodore Roetke

"Wherever you are is the entry point"
- Kabir

So many things were in play during the months after Allen's passing. As I write this, I'll sometimes go back and forth in time a bit in order to tell it all. Even though I'd had some extraordinary events in those early days after his death, many I've already talked about were yet to come. So at first, I felt like a novice on a path I'd never travelled before. Yes, I'd lost relatives, such as my beloved Grandpa when I was young, but I had never lost anyone this close to me. My whole world was changed in one brief October afternoon.

I thought I was getting by, until Jim noticed my change in behavior. Where once I had dealt with bad drivers by saying, "Bless you, and send you on your way," - and then had imagined protective white light around their car and mine, and the other cars they would meet on the road, I started taking a different tack. One day, when my irritation at these rude drivers now showed in my voice, Jim tactfully said, "Mom, maybe it would be good for you to go to a Grief Group now."

He saw my unresponsive attitude.

"You know," he wisely reframed his thought, "I think we both need to go."

I looked at him, my eyes softer now.

"I'll go with you, Mom." He took my hand. "It will be good for both of us."

"Am I starting to act different?"

"Yeah, Mom, you kinda are." His eyes softened too. "But it's understandable."

We knew people like our dear friends, Connie, Paulina and Lisa, who had done so, and it had helped them. It wasn't a sign of weakness or inability to figure things out on your own, we decided. Especially because of their example, we knew it was a sign of strength. A sign of being wise.

Grief can be lonely business. Even if you are processing stuff, you can begin to feel like a hermit. And sometimes while you are deeply dealing with internal things, you can *become* a hermit. It makes sense, because you actually need time alone, to think. But it is a heavy load to handle on your own.

During the first week of grieving, I went out with a friend to look at a church for Allen's service. The Unity Church we visited had a wonderful bookstore and I picked up their pocket size magazine. In it, I read a story about a woman who grieved. She felt she was the only one who had suffered this kind of loss. She grieved and grieved, feeling entirely alone in her grief. Then some wise person gently suggested she go to the village and knock on each door, and ask if someone there had grieved a devastating loss.

She immediately took up the challenge, knowing still that she was the only one who had grieved this deeply. But as she knocked on door after door, her heart changed. She discovered that almost everyone had suffered a devastating loss. And knowing she was not alone somehow opened her heart, and her real healing began.

That's why I wrote the poem at the beginning of this book, "Humanity's Cares." We are all part of a big circle. When pain walks in, as it will do, we may see our connection with all who have suffered, and become . . .

> *softened by humanity's cares,*
> *more acutely aware*
> *more compassionately aware*
> *more kindly aware*
> *of the Heart we all share.*

I remember one "Write Your Life Stories" class I taught. As you hear people's stories, you begin to understand all of us have suffered. But one person seemed untouched by loss. She dressed impeccably and always had positive stories. That is, until one day she wrote about her son being sexually molested by her husband, thus the reason for her divorce! And another woman who was also always so positive seemed untouched by suffering, but after a long and wonderful marriage, her husband had died. These are losses, real losses, and over the course of time, they leave no one untouched.

All this is how I felt when I started attending the Grief Group, thankfully given for free at a nearby hospital.

My opening up didn't start all at once. The facilitator went around in a circle and asked each of us to say something. All of us were being pretty careful until one day, when a man joined the group and immediately said, "Hey, are any of you experiencing what I am?"

"What's that?" we asked.

"Well, my late wife is around me. In fact, she touched my shoulder. Aren't all of you feeling something like this?" His right brow went up, to accentuate the question. I loved his open, assumptive nature as he requested our responses.

I still chuckle at how this analytical, professional man opened up our grief group. Suddenly everyone sighed, relieved they could talk about the mystical, "hard-to-talk-about-in-our-society" things that were happening - and how it was helping them.

In one moment of sharing, we no longer felt alone. "Maybe this is doable, after all," I thought.

At the same time, one of the writer-friends from my publishing group said something that struck me. Nancy said, "Sheila, you should write about all this. You should get a journal, and write it down." She had gone through loss and suffering, and she was a good listener with a kind heart. "You should start writing again."

An avid writer and meditator, I had no longer been able to do either of these things after Allen's passing over, so I wasn't processing some of the things that were happening, much less my feelings about them. I am eternally thankful to Nancy.

"When we write, we figure things out."
- Sheila Stephens

I remember the first thing I wrote, which I then shared with the grief group. I quickly decided that even though I was a professional writer, I wouldn't try to be one when I wrote these poems now. I had to write from my gut. As Jim so wisely knew, I had to get it out. I've lost my first journal, but the first poem revolved honestly around the utter pain I was feeling, and it ended with an authentic statement that helped me tremendously:

I feel like a two-year old,
stamping her feet,
trying to say
"I just want everyone to know
how much I loved him!"

That was the essence of it for me. In all my grieving and in all my actions, that's what I was really trying to say.

It made me ask myself, "So what are you going to do with that?"

It made me do two things: 1) it made me give voice to how I loved Allen; and 2) it made me love and honor myself, by giving voice to all my feelings.

Secret Number 13:
Let your voice be heard.
It will clear the skies
and mend your Heart -
by leading you into the Extraordinary.

One of the next things I wrote was about was socks. An ordinary thing? - Yes. But our days are made up of ordinary things, and sometimes we find our grief caught up in them. So extricating them by pulling them up to look at them can be surprisingly healing. I wrote about finding one of Allen's socks in my laundry basket after he had passed. It hit me hard, this one sock. *It was no longer part of a pair.*

Alone in my bedroom, folding laundry, I wept as I held the one sock in my hand. No one was there to see my tears - but now, as I wrote about it, I had given it light. Somehow I had shared it. And I found it helped me breathe.

I also wrote about the visits from the first hawk during Christmas.

"Journey with the Red-Tailed Hawk"

Oh that my fingers will begin to move again;
oh that my heart will unlock its mysteries
and tell me how to live, to step,
to gaze once again
with joy.

I know that you are now
merely invisible to mine eyes -
mine eyes that look inward now,
upon myself,
and see only a bird that flies alone -
but you send me the Red-Tailed Hawk,
spirit bird that flies through my loneliness,
that perches like a resolute
statue of irrevocable love -
perches here, in the midst of my path,
on power lines over our hometown highway
that never held a hawk within my sight before.
That sent its presence to remind me of one week ago:
Same place on highway's door.
Same place that opened
when wings rose from the meridian
and flashed and swooped
unabashed,
across my sight

changing my inner sight
evermore.

No more distance separating two birds
that hear the brush of wings,
and bridge two worlds.

My love, you have Red-Tailed Hawk's
strong gift that moves with hush
between the Veil -
to call me into the grand expanse of life -
the poetry of flight,
the gentle skies of love's devotion
now the chosen course.

Writing helped me both to communicate my feelings (which not everyone understands unless they have suffered the loss of a Loved One), and to understand my feelings. I read the poem about the Red-Tailed Hawk at Christmas with family, and it felt good to share it and also to acknowledge Allen, even though he wasn't physically present. I also was able to read some of these poems to the Grief Group and to friends. Each time, it helped me. It gave me a major outlet to be heard.

During the process, I was even able to take the innermost feelings I'd had, about wanting to go out and sit under a fir tree to die after Allen had passed over, to the loving and understanding arms of the members of my Grief Group. After getting me started, Jim was no longer going with me. At some point, it helped just to give voice to what was lodged like a stone, so deeply in my heart. These were things I did not want to admit to my children, of course. I felt blessed by the words of response I heard from our grief counselor. She said that *many* people feel this way. It was a completely normal reaction, and was something she heard often. What a relief this was to me! Her words of compassion breathed air into my tight, hunkered-down emotions, and I relaxed a bit, knowing I could stay on this planet and live a life that helped my children. Because of being part of this group, I had extricated part of my pain. I had identified it. I had shared it with someone else. And now I had room to let it go.

As I understood and honored my feelings more and more, I also was more able to receive. I started seeing how Spirit was surrounding my heart with Love, by bringing in these extraordinary events to help me heal. Somehow I think all of this works in tandem - our honesty and receptivity allows the Divine Universe to bring Light into the darkness, and give us wings.

After some of this writing and some of these gifted experiences, I went in to see my Chinese acupuncturist, Dr. "Joe," as we call him. Actually Dr. Zhou, but he doesn't care about how you pronounce it. As I relaxed on the acupuncture table, Dr. Joe came in to see me. He touched my arm, ever so gently, and said with the most compassionate eyes I've ever seen, "I'm so sorry for your loss. You really love your husband."

Dr. Joe knew both Allen and myself, and his kind words soaked into my soul.

"How are you?" he asked, as he patiently stopped seeing other patients so he could give me all the time I needed.

"I am all right," I said, meaning it.

He looked deeply into my eyes - and heart.

"I know Allen is just on the Other Side of the Veil," I said. "Kind of like this light curtain." I gestured to the curtain that divided each client and gave them privacy. "I feel the curtain is so thin - just a whisper."

He smiled, his all-knowing smile. "Yes, the Veil is very thin."

"It's gossamer." I smiled, too, and wasn't ashamed of the tears that went with it.

"That's how we feel, too," he said, also meaning it.

"Yes," I answered him. And we both knew I was going to be all right. I loved his gentle, whole-hearted smile. Dr. Joe is like a version of the Dalai Lama, right here amongst us.

It was a healing moment, and one reason it came into being was because I had been writing, and writing was giving me a voice, a new kind of voice - a voice that honored the extraordinary.

How I took the leap from socks to the gossamer Veil seems a bit funny now, but if we value each step of healing (including how bad we feel when we find a solo sock!), we will actually heal better. Even today, 10 years later, if I feel a sadness, I will give voice to it. And often my sons just hug me. In a beautiful way, it helps them, too. We're in it together, and have become an even closer family because of the way we've handled our grieving.

I wrote a poem about Julian, who biologically is my stepson, but who definitely feels like a real son through and through, to me. His physical stature reminds me of his dad's:

"In Your Shoulders"

Julian, in your shoulders
I see your father,
and in your hug
you bring him back home to me.

It is a great gift you give us.
The hug of a man we all love
in the hug
of a man we love.

This brings up another concept that works wonders for me:

Secret Number 14:
Speak of your Loved Ones
in the Present Tense when you can,
for they are Alive in spirit.

On the day Allen died, I had trouble saying, "Allen *was* a good man" - because I knew he *is* a good man (whether on this side of the Veil, or the Other Side of it). Likewise, I had trouble saying, "I loved him" - because I still love him. As I had extraordinary experiences, I learned more and more how right my impulse was - to speak in the present tense when it feels right.

It changes everything. It shifts the energy. And as it does that, it harmonizes with the Divine Universe. And this shift in energy allows your Loved One in, to tend your heart, and gently let you know you are never alone. When you try it, it really works. It always makes my heart happy when I say IS instead of WAS, and I express how I LOVE HIM, instead of how I loved him. (It's important to note: you don't have to be perfect and always use the present tense though. Sometimes it is appropriate to use the past tense. In using the present tense, we are not trying to deny "death," but we are affirming the Lifeforce of their spirit on the Other Side.)

Once we start changing things to the present tense, we can take the next step. It changes the energy in a huge way when, *instead of saying "I miss him," we say "I love him."* This change is huge. Try it. The shift inherent in these few emotional words of expression has a positive ripple affect that allows your heart to open to Spirit, and listen with a beautiful innocence. It also helps you to start celebrating your Loved One:

"White Cherry Blossoms"

My love,
you are like
the snow crystals
dancing in the night sky.
No branches needed.

With this cherishing of your Loved One, you also start receiving more gifts from the loving Universe, more Ah-Ha's. You might even look at the Moon differently . . .

Chapter Nine

The Full Moon

As I walked my path of healing, it was becoming more and more mystical. *I think mystical must mean: holding the mysteries.* Because that is what these miraculous events do - they hold the mysteries until you are ready for them to reveal themselves.

The night before Allen died, he called me. His job required him to work late every night, and he liked keeping in touch. Anyway, that night he called and said, "Go outside before I come home, honey. Go outside and see the moon right now."

It was late. I was tired. And I was bundled up for the night, slippers and all. But I was taken by Allen's excitement - and his rare insistence - so I went out our front door. Because of this, I was able to see *the last moon, that in some mystical way, announced his upcoming death: the beautiful, glowing moon was in eclipse!*

The next day, Allen crossed over. That night it was a Full Moon.

I started noticing the Full Moon every month, and writing about it. In an inexplicable way, it helped me heal, and it brought more messages from the Other Side. This is one of those poems from the first part of my journey:

"The Other Side of the Moon"

Some nights,
when the drum beats softly,
it's time to sit on the other side of the moon.
Some nights,
it is right to remember
the eternal warrior I am,

the eternal warrior who fights for love;
who remembers love;
who IS love -
who is love from before the dawn breaks,
when stars still guide the dreams
and awaken dreamers
to the fast connections
of the heart.

Some nights
I need to sit with you, my love,
not just meet you half way,
but remember my eternal self,
at home when the drum beats
as I sit on the other side of the moon,
my heart in your heart -
the eternal warrior in me
finding its way back to the truth -
no separation.
no veil.
just the two of us -
one heart, at home
on the other side of the moon.

Quite quickly, something interrelated and quite organic started happening. In one of my first short poems about the Full Moon (I lost the first journal it was in), I was missing Allen. Then, as I watched the moon and wrote about it each month, I began realizing he was with me. In a mystical way, the Full Moon was somehow nudging me forward.

Other fascinating synchronicities started happening. When I went out on my first major public outing after his passing, a song played as I was trying to find a parking space near the KATU-TV studio. Our publishing group was visiting the set to be on a popular local talk show, AM-NW, and promote an upcoming writing event. I was painfully aware I was going solo. I was also aware of how, just weeks ago, I had turned off my cell phone when I attended the meeting of that publishers' group the morning Allen was killed. It was the reason we hadn't been able to stay in touch that day, and by the time I turned my cell phone back on after the meeting, he was no longer answering. He was gone.

So I was pretty tense as I hurried to find a parking place, and tried to get to the TV studio on time. Reality was caving in on me, and then I heard it - the song by Bonnie Tyler that emotionally stopped me in tracks. As I drove around the block, her song reminded me about how losing Allen was like the "Total Eclipse of the Heart!"

I was the last one from our publishers' group to arrive at the studio, but, although shaken, I arrived with a bit of grace in my pocket. Allen often called me Bright Eyes, as I now heard in the song. I felt Allen's spirit reminding me how, if I just turned around (or gained a new perspective), I would understand he was with me. Love never leaves. It just takes a different form. And if I was willing, he would show me how to keep receiving that beautiful, gentle love - a love capable of sustaining me and lifting me up through difficult times. Over the years, I would come to hear that beautiful love song about the total eclipse of the heart at the most opportune moments. Always when I needed it most.

Secret Number 15:
*As you share and listen with others who have suffered,
it will open up a Circle of Compassion
that brings more healing to all.*

As the months passed - and as I wrote about my experiences - a series of healings occurred within my heart. The Full Moon became not a sign of sorrow, but a sign of Allen's presence with me. And the appearance of the Red-Tailed Hawks no longer stood as a single event, but made me open up to spirit visits from other animals. And my suffering became not just my own suffering, but part of the Circle of Humanity's suffering. *A Circle of Compassion.* The Grief Group helped me see how I was a part of an even greater group, and that instructed my heart. As I progressed, Allen's spirit infused me with a greater perspective, a greater compassion, and a greater purpose.

"Full Moon"

Allen died on a Full Moon,
the day after an eclipse.
Tonight, 9 months later,
the evening of the Full Moon arrives
and I hold my breath,
still not wanting to remember.
But he fills the muggy July evening
with a painter's flourish of riotous red skies
and pink light on the houses
as the sun sets.
Then, not to be mistaken,
lightning at 1 A.M. -
noticeable even behind my closed eyelids!
I flick on the lamp to write
under the mystical drama of the Full Moon.
Then thunder -
big whopping bolts
that only visit the Summer skies of kids.
More lightning again.
Then the loudest rush
of pelting rain.
Finally I'm laughing.
"OK, I get it!", I murmur
with a lighter heart -
I'm the rain, laughing.
I'm the lightning of Allen,
zapping the strength of love
between two dimensions.
And I'm the sky of the Full Moon,
receiving the creative gifts
of my best friend.

I would think about the Full Moon often as I opened up my spirit to new ways of receiving and healing. One of the biggest gifts

I received from what I call "the expansiveness of moon-time" was through Dreams. But other ways of spacious connecting wove through this beautiful tapestry of hints and insights from the Other Side.

Secret Number 16:
Your Loved Ones will use creative ways to reach you:
The Radio, TV, Flickering Lights, Dreams, and more!
Get a Journal, and Write them Down.

As I eventually put my new learnings into practice, I taught a class on grieving, entitled *"Healing from Grief: Don't Let Your Loved One Go; Let Your Loved One In."* The students reflected a wide range of experiences, and most had received some communications from their departed Loved Ones. People talked about how their lights were suddenly flickering, some by the bed, or some on light poles. It happened at very distinct and weird times. One person called the electric company quite a few times, but the light on the nearby pole was just fine. I myself had the lamp on Allen's side of the bed repaired. Where previously it was in perfect condition, after his death it started flickering - quite dramatically. Then there was contact by radio (like the "Total Eclipse of the Heart" song), and more. Many people reported this form of very precise, personal contact from their Loved Ones, including my friend, Lisa, who had lost her brother. Her eyes brightened (ahh, "bright eyes"), when she spoke of it.

These cosmic connections often happen easily, even when we're not expecting them, but sometimes we don't feel the connection. One nice woman felt especially cut off from her beloved husband who had passed over. "He is dead, and that's that," she stated adamantly. There was nothing else. But after hearing of other students' "happenings," she wondered about connecting.

"He doesn't come to me in dreams, or in any way," she still stated flatly, but there was a whisper of desire in it. So I asked her how she liked to communicate to people in ordinary life. Her eyes brightened up (yahoo!) as she talked about how she loved to write letters. She was a giving woman, and confessed she wrote beautiful letters.

"How about doing that then?" The kind, very intelligent woman looked at me quizzically. "How about writing your late husband a letter?" I added.

She was a can-do person, so at the next class she sat down and leaned forward to tell me and the class how she'd written her husband a letter.

"How did you feel about that?" I queried, opening it up so she could tell us anything she wanted to share.

"He came to me in a dream!" she beamed. "He visited me." It had made her exceedingly happy, and it made the whole class happy as the loving, gentle force of her smiled swept through all of us.

This beautiful, unexpected event underlines the power of reaching out, and asking, and also clarifies how *writing is a magical medium*, in all its forms, from personal letters, to journals, to poems and stories and essays. It can be used to break through some of our blocks and our resistance during all our stages of grieving. As all of us in our class took time out from our regular lives to share our unique experiences, we found we were all helping each other. One person's experiences helped the other, and vice versa.

It seems all of us, each in our own time, were being given a foundation from which to start opening to more communication with our Loved Ones. With my own experiences tucked under my wings, my dreams began in earnest, and they would prove to change me - from the inside, out. From moon-time, to day-time. These dreams deepened and were more than mere dreams, they were a stunning series of visitations, and I would learn from each and every one of them.

"Beside Us at the Table"

In one of my first dreams, Jim, Julian, and myself were in a house. We were all together, doing stuff. We were in mourning, and so we were moving around as if in a fog, but we were there for each other. Together. *And Allen was there, too!* He was sitting at the dining room table, right in the middle of us - but we didn't know it. We didn't see him. In the dream, I walked right by him, and tried to help my sons. But now he was showing me he was there, beside me in spirit, helping me get through any of the tough stuff I was feeling. Helping all of us do that. It was a mighty dream. I remember feeling stunned by it. "You're actually here with us," I realized.

"Even When You Feel Alone, I am There"

Because of my journal beside my bed, I wrote these dreams down, and I started having many dreams in which Allen visited me. In the beginning, or when I was under stress, I had dreams of being in an apartment, alone. Allen was at work, or was going to work, and I felt as if I was imprisoned in a way. I was in a box I couldn't get out of. These were painful dreams, but Allen was showing me he was there - always with me, watching over me. Again and again, in so many different ways, he would show me how he was there, even when I felt most alone. It happened so often, I had to open my heart to let it all in.

That began to change me, like I said, from the inside, out.

As I learned to let Allen be with me in a different way, I wrote:

"The Secret of Foxgloves"

*The secret of Foxgloves
is their seeds.
Just as you think
the foxglove's flowers
have died, and are done,
you cut off a branch
and hold it,
and for some unknown reason,
you decide to shake it -
only to hear the seeds
of new growth
fast within!*

*You shake them lovingly
to the ground,*

and whisper their Song.

The Foxgloves smile
and give you their
Harmony -
as they sing back to you
their sonorous notes
of Thankfulness.

I can hear Allen saying that he loves being called Sonorous! His joy makes me smile all over again. And I'm thinking - maybe I'm actually learning how to give back to him now.

I just turned on my TV. The talk show host is a woman. She's saying: "I love paying attention to my dreams." Funny, isn't it? - how all this synchronicity works! Once we start paying attention to our dreams, some dreams can lead us to other dream-like, mystical happenings in our real lives. In the most beautiful, everyday-kind-of-way, as in the heart-opening experience with the Foxgloves - *healing finds a way.*

Secret Number 17:
Work Lovingly with your Dreams.

Here are some DREAM TIPS to help you. If you work with your Dreams *lovingly,* you show your appreciation of the gifts and insights your Loved One and Higher Spirit want to bring to you - special delivery.

1. If you want your Loved One to visit you, do your part by setting the stage. *Just before you go to sleep, think of your Loved One who has passed over.* Think of happy memories with them. And invite them to visit you.

2. Dreams often come in just before you wake up, so *let yourself slumber in this half-awake, dreamy state for 10-20 minutes in*

the morning. You'll find more dreams settle in and give you their whole message. They often take time to complete themselves then.

3. *Keep a journal beside your bed* or even under your pillow. You'll capture many dreams that otherwise would have floated away - especially in the morning time.

4. *Thank your Loved One for visiting. And thank Higher Spirit for bringing your Loved One to you.*

5. Honor your Loved One's visit by *incorporating the wisdoms and Love within these dreams into your everyday life.* They'll notice.

6. *Do NOT complain about not receiving a dream right away.* Stay in a positive higher energy about it, and keep inviting them to visit you in your dreams. *Patience is a part of Love.* Also, your Loved One is being patient as they wait for you to open your heart to receive.

7. It's been scientifically documented that everyone dreams, especially in deep REM states. Just know that if you aren't able to be aware of your dreams or remember them, *your Loved One will find another way to visit you - if you but ask.* The Divine Universe is a highly creative place!

But also try to remember your dreams. They are an unparalleled gift in the way in which they break through our conscious, more limited thoughts.

8. Use your journal to *note the ways your Loved One seems near.* Also *start writing down the Wisdoms you are receiving* (as in #5). The act of writing underlines the Visitations and Wisdoms - and says to the Universe, you're ready for more.

Not every dream will be worthy of note or worthy of remembering. Don't dwell on ones you don't find helpful (especially dreams that come when you're sick). *Concentrate on the dreams that are helpful and have value.*

All of this will help you with your growth. You are finding a way to expand into Love - into More Love. You are noticing the Seeds of Opportunity strewn along your path. You are doing honor to Love.

And that will make your Loved One feel sonorous!

Secret Number 18:
Let the healing power of Nature tend you.

Over the years after Allen's passing, I came to appreciate Nature's healing touch even more. Amongst many other gifts from Nature, month by month, the mystical nature of the Full Moon bloomed into my everyday life. Looking back in my journals, I found these two poems that, although written on the same night, explore different aspects of an event with Nature. They were written the year *before* Allen's passing. Like "Sacred Preparations," I found they reflected some of the transitions I was going through the first year on my journey of healing from grief.

This first poem reminds me of some of the early stages of healing:

> *Full moon rises high*
> *in midnight blue November sky.*
> *Clouds glow in the light.*

And this poem reminds me of deeper stages of healing and understanding that came in afterward:

> *"Blossom Moon"*
>
> *butter-white full moon*
> *moves high against November's*
> *sky - stopping only to bloom.*

In these poems, I felt Allen's spirit blooming. And I also felt mine beginning to do the same then. As I write this, I'm stunned to remember something so obvious to me - I think, how could I leave this out?! The stunningly beautiful, evocative, romantic thing I want to tell you, is that Allen and I first met right after I felt a distinct pull from the Full Moon. Single then, I had gone out on my deck, and stood under its luminous beauty. Something nudged me to remember a saying, "It's good to make a wish under a Full Moon." So that night I said, "Why not?!" - and I asked for the right man to come into my life.

Two days after that request under the Full Moon, I surprisingly met Allen when I went to pick up my young son, Jim, from my ex, and people watched as "something happened." The link between our hearts was instantaneous, and that week began a lifetime love. I'm glad my sweetheart was coming to me once again - through the powerful sway and the healing light of our Full Moon. It's fun to see that evocative, poetic parallel unfold into my consciousness now, too.

It's amazing to me - how Nature offers us images and scenes that evoke a deeper personal meaning within us - and a more profound healing. So, too, do dreams and events. As Nature's Loving inner sight opened me to accept its graceful type of ministries, several dreams revolving around my dear Allen captured my complete attention. They coupled effortlessly with some extremely magical events, and to this day, make *me* feel sonorous.

They put the puzzle pieces together in a way I can never forget.

Chapter Ten

Puzzle Pieces

Belvedere: a structure designed to command a view

Sometimes you want a perch, a tree house, or a grand gazebo in a place that offers you a higher view - along with a higher perspective.   Helpful Dreams do that.   And so do Exceptional Events.   They are our Belvederes.   These higher quality dreams and events give us a vantage point that increases our vision and brings a peaceful balance to our days as we integrate them into our consciousness, and into our daily reality.

Having a perch can give us both a wider perspective, which allows us to look further than before, and it can show us the small things, the details that are like puzzle pieces. As these small things fit together, we start to see the beautiful design these puzzle pieces create. *Our lives are works of art, being formed and revealed, each in its own pace. At the pace of Love. In this way, the Veil is lifted, event by event over time. This is one reason healing takes time.* We are meant to learn and take it all in. The "healing" is actually our "growth." Healing from grief is not just about "getting over it;" it's about "getting better." The Mystery School of Grief wants you to come out of the experience as a better person, with a more expanded soul, and it will pull-out-the-stops to help you achieve this higher perspective of who you can become. And our Loved Ones will help! Spirit designed it that way, and what a great gift from Spirit this is.

As I wondered what example to start with, I reached back, across an antique marble table behind me, to put some stick 'em notes away, and my fingers touched something. As I looked to see what it was, I saw the cool, realistic, 12" long metal toy replica of a Schwan's truck - rolling wheels and all - that Allen had been given at work years ago. It's just like the one Allen drove! And here it was, rolling toward me!

So, I begin with the Schwan's truck . . .

It began quite some time ago, and much as the Full Moon had brought Allen and myself together and wove its way through our life, so, too, did the Schwan's truck weave its way through our life. The Full Moon came first, of course, but about 4 years before Allen's death, he was making a transition from having his own business (our communications and advertising agency) to getting a new job with a company. Companies wouldn't even give him a job interview, as no one seemed to think he would stick with it, since he'd been so independent for 15 years. But I was very sick at the time and we needed the security of a regular job. I had almost died from a toxic overload pertaining to dental silver point pins used in root canals in the early 70's, and it was a tough time for us. So Allen applied to Schwan's, but was nervous about it. He'd never been a truck driver, much less had to memorize the huge inventory codes a full service food delivery company required. So we decided to pray about it. Well, I asked *him* to pray about it, because I knew it was pretty much going to work out.

Since we had a bit of time, we travelled to Montana to research a Western novel Allen was working on. As we drove up, we saw the nice bed and breakfast, and were happy with our choice. But we very quickly noticed one very obvious thing. In front of this great B & B was parked a large, yellow truck - a Schwan's truck at that! I laughed and stated the obvious, "Yes, you certainly received your answer to prayer!" Allen took a deep breath and started figuring out how to memorize a zillion food product codes!

When we arrived back in town a week later, Schwan's called like clockwork and offered him the job. Allen accepted, but still, memorizing all the codes was hard!

Allen's Schwan's truck route proved to be a God-send. As he travelled through Hillsboro, he developed a following of friends. He stopped along his way to have heart-felt and uplifting conversations with people of diverse faiths and philosophies. As I've said, at his Celebration of Life, I understood his great Purpose during the last years of his life. They loved him, and he loved them. He did things no one knew about except me, like when he bought food from his own budget so a single mom did not have to go without. And he talked one woman out of committing suicide. And he grieved with families when a man lost his wife, or a woman lost her husband. These friendships were his riches, and they also helped make him the man he was, because they offered the beauty of serving. He served from his heart.

So after Allen passed over, I started seeing Schwan's trucks where I'd only seen a handful before then. They would wiz by at times I was under stress. Spirit wants me to reiterate this. Again and again, our Loved Ones visit us when we need them. So they tend to surprise us, again and again, usually at our moments of vulnerability. I won't even be thinking of Allen when it happens. It happened even this week!

One day I was particularly stressed out. After Allen died, I had to regain the rest of my health, and because of the silver toxicity, it was hard. It lingered in my body for years, and I eventually went through a year and a half of a specialized form of NAET acupuncture designed to neutralize various things your particular body reacts badly to. My list was long, but I forged ahead.

That morning I had to go to a hospital 45 minutes away for a blood test. I didn't feel well (a condition that would come and go for years), and I hadn't been able to drink coffee or eat anything yet. I was truly on my last legs. I'd even had to turn around half way there to go back and get my blood test request. So here I was, on my second trip.

I blinked when I saw it. Up in front of me and to my right, was a Schwan's truck. I beamed and blinked, and beamed and blinked again - for right beside the front door of the Schwan's truck stood my dear Allen . . .

He was waving at me!

He was smiling that big, heart-warming smile of his!

I cried and smiled, and cried and smiled.

And just as quickly, Allen faded away . . . and I saw only the truck.

I still mist up, just telling you about this. I couldn't believe it, really. I had actually seen Allen - in real life! He had somehow come through the Veil, and brought himself to me in full color. Blue Schwan's shirt and all.

This is how Allen was in life, he was proud to step up and be there for me and our family. He liked a Michael Bolton song, called "Soul Provider" (notice how it's spelled), and came home one day, asking me to listen to it. I give him an A+ for how he's done it from the Other Side. And we really needed all he has given us.

Allen was there for me, now both as a real life vision, and also in my dreams, but one dream especially stays with me and continues to tell me a lot.

"The Fire & the Friendly Conference Room"

In the dream, my house was on fire and I was in it. Allen came to be with me, and he guided me out of the fire. But at the same time, he brought me my favorite black velvet robe with beautiful gold quilted trim. He was taking care of me in all kinds of way. He wanted to get me out of the fire, but he also wanted to comfort me and protect me from the elements.

Then he paused and invited me to join him for a while if I wanted.

I obviously said Yes, so he guided me down a wide corridor, and into a comfortable conference room. He told me I could sit down in a big office chair.

At that moment, I realized I was on the Other Side! I watched as some wonderful people came in. They were very warm and friendly to me, as they smiled and rolled their chairs up to the round conference table beside me. Allen introduced me right away, and everyone made me feel so welcome, like I was an honored guest - which indeed I was!

What happened next surprised me and pleased me.

Allen went to the front of the conference room and gave a presentation about the things he had learned.

On the Other Side, Allen was teaching! Which told me that we continue to learn, and continue to share, both in roles of students and teachers, on the Other Side.

So in this beautiful dream, Allen had protected me (from the fire), comforted me (with my robe), and taken me on a trip of a lifetime - to the Other Side!

For obvious reason, I have loved and remembered this dream. It certainly was a belvedere of sacred proportions, giving a much more expanded perspective than I'd ever had before. Within the dream was another thing that meant the world to me. Within the dream, I felt Allen's love. It was warm and devoted, just as Allen was in his dedication to his family here on Earth. It was and is a treasured moment - when you feel that love full-force in a dream. It's a kind of love without strings. It's as if he's a Spirit Guide to me now, helping me forge new relationships and encouraging me to follow my bliss so I might fulfill my Purposes here on Earth.

Many dreams, like this one, feel more real than just a dream. This is the case with a Visitation Dream. They are exquisite, and can be applied in many ways to our daily lives.

Secret Number 19:
Visitation Dreams
hold a beauty all their own.
Let their Love & Inspiration change your Perspective.

One of the gifts I received from this Visitation Dream was how I no longer felt alone. Each one of Allen's Visitation Dreams did this for me - and there were many. I also decided to do something just a little bold because of it. On a visit to a contemporary art exhibit at the Portland Art Museum, I saw a booth. It looked much like a phone booth, only the artist had filled it with black hanging pieces of fabric. There were so many of them, that when you stepped in, you had no vision. It literally blocked out all light. It was indeed a Black Box.

It was an interesting experience of feeling alone. It's nice to challenge ourselves. This kind of sensory deprivation took me away from all my ordinary crutches in life. No furniture, no light, no people. How would a person react when everything is stripped away? You may ask yourself, "Who am I?"

But more importantly, you may ask a deeper question, "Who do I want to be (in this experience)?"

As I faced the darkness inside the Black Box, I found I had taken something in with me: it was a great peace. In some way, through everything I had experienced, including Allen's visitations in my dreams, I DID NOT FEEL ALONE.

It's fascinating to note that in painting, the color Black contains ALL the colors.

It was a most beautiful, serene feeling, and I was glad I had pushed myself to go in it, so I could have this solo experience - with no parachute, so to speak.

Oddly enough, this coincides with something I found in a Dream Dictionary by Tony Crisp. Usually these guides and interpretations are not at all what I rely on. I've learned a person's personal feeling of what things in a dream mean are more accurate and meaningful. But I liked this definition. It simply says:

ALONE = All One.

There are many ways we end up feeling All One instead of alone. One big ah-ha moment happened when I was editing Allen's Western during the first year after his passing. As I edited the first chapter, I realized something that made me stop in my tracks:

Allen's hero in his novel (the protagonist) had died the same way Allen had -
with a blow to the head - to the temple, in fact!

Allen had many injuries, but the blow to his temple was the big one, the cause of his death. In his book, Allen's hero, Jake, had been riding his horse, celebrating with friends after they found a lot of gold in his goldmine. Jake was shot, so there were minor differences, but being killed by a blow to the temple was an amazing parallel.

I immediately started wondering if it was the same temple. I read and read, and then finally I saw it. Allen's hero, Jake, was killed by a bullet in the right temple - the very same side as Allen!

This also paired with another incredible fact. Allen had been writing this book, his Western adventure, about a man who had been killed, and then passed over to the Other Side. Allen wrote this the final year before his death.

In "Gone to Glory," Jake is sent back - to live his life with all he had learned from the Other Side. So Jake lived it differently than before, and throughout the book, his hero kept receiving intuitive guidance, and had to learn how to absorb a higher vision and work it into his life.

As I edited Allen's fine book, these synchronicities, insights, and parallels helped me see the Weaving of Allen's destiny. I knew none of us are ever alone.

At times when I have lived "alone," I say instead: "I am on my own - with a lot of help!" At these times, I feel surrounded by Angels and Spirit Guides who bring Divine Love into my heart and into my days. Indeed, we are never really alone.

One more exceptional event stands out in my memory. It was a real event:

"Puzzle Pieces - the Event"

One night I heard an unfamiliar noise, so I got out of bed and made my way to the family room. Boy, was I shocked! *In front of me, sitting in the recliner - was Allen!* This was not a dream. This was real. He was sitting in his favorite burgundy leather recliner, the one he had sat in every morning when we had our coffee together.

As I stared in disbelief, I realized he looked different. It was just *part* of him that I was seeing. Part of his torso, his nice broad shoulders, and his head. I recognized him even further because of his hair. I had always cut his hair, and I knew every strand of it. And it was most assuredly him. (This is called a "tell" because this detail was his way of "telling" me it was him!) I was so glad, so very, very glad to see him!

He looked so vibrant and alive. Then something further happened. I noticed his being was like a picture puzzle. I could see the puzzle pieces very clearly. I knew it was his spirit, come to me for this glorious visit.

The feeling from his heart radiated out - into every part of me. It was so warm and generous as his spirit bonded with mine, and lovingly tended me. It was the same radiant glow I had felt when Allen first passed over.

As I realized this, the puzzle pieces started to gently fall away, bit by bit, as if they were disappearing through my fingertips.

And then his spirit was no longer there . . .

I stood there in my nightgown for the longest time, while the cat sat calmly on the chair, trying to convince me she wasn't the cause of the night's noise.

How can you really describe something like this - and what it does to your heart? There is no way. All I can say is that even as I write it now, I cry *good tears*.

I deeply appreciate how Allen showed me I wasn't alone.

Several years later, I was dating a fine man, my friend John, in Camp Sherman. As we walked the lovely trails along the Metolius River, I was taken by something on the Ponderosa Pine trees. It is called "puzzle bark" - Ponderosa puzzle bark. This glorious, strong pine tree's outer layer of bark is made up of just puzzle pieces which fit together in the most amazing of designs. Often times, they lay at the base of the tree, announcing the great tree by the cluster of their delicate pieces.

Chapter Eleven

Fabulous Feathers, Felines, and Friends

At a conference I attended this weekend, people noticed my hawk necklace one day, and my dragonfly necklace the next day. As we talked about how they symbolized the spirit of my late husband being with me, many people instantly started sharing their stories, as if they had been yearning to speak about them. Sometimes we hold these precious events in our hearts for a long time before we get a chance to speak about them.

The first example that came up was about Pennies from Heaven! I had to consciously keep my jaw from dropping. One kind woman had lost her brother recently and she was finding pennies everywhere. She was very conversant with the subject. "I even find them at the park. In fact, I found a whole lovely pile of them!"

She had our attention. Someone asked her how many there were.

"Well, let's see . . . I was so taken by them, I took a photo," she added. Then with an oh-my-God expression on her face, the woman exclaimed, "Look, I have the photo with me!"

As she retrieved her handy cell phone from her purse, her nimble fingers quickly rolled through the photos until she found her treasured snapshot. All of us literally said, "Ohhhhhh," as we saw the shiny cluster of pretty pennies. I really had never seen anything like it. No one had. It was as if they were beautifully placed there, purposely.

"What did you do with them?" someone asked.

"I had received my message, so I left them there. I left them there to bless someone else," she answered and gently smiled, her eyes shining with those bright eyes we've become so accustomed to seeing when people talk about caring signs from their Loved Ones.

The conversation turned to other signs. People were sharing stories with me about Pennies from Heaven, dragonflies, butterflies, rainbows, and all kinds of birds (including hawks) that seemed to convey a message from their Loved Ones - including one sign I'd forgotten about - feathers. Once again, this gentle woman was an "angel" to me. As she shared her story about feathers, it made me further appreciate my experience with my wonderful cat, Aquarius.

Everyone loved Aquarius, from the moment we saw her, to the moment she passed. She captured everyone's hearts, whether they were family or strangers. We had plenty of fun outside, as she "helped me" with my gardening, but she also curled up with me during the time when I had almost died from a toxic dental overload. She walked the long path with me as if she was glued to me. I couldn't have asked for a kinder, sweeter kitty-cat.

My beautiful, gentle Aquarius died at the lofty age of 18. She died in my arms at the vets, and after Allen and I sent her off with our love, we went outside. I remember standing on the sidewalk, as tears racked my body. I had trouble making it to the car, which was right beside me.

Before Aquari (as we called her) passed, the boys came to spend Christmas with us, and they knew her time was nigh. Aquari was very sick, but it was as if she waited for everyone to come home. When we opened presents, she was in the middle of all of us as we sat on the living room floor, touching each of us with her nose, or walking on the Christmas wrapping paper to plop down on our laps. We all took time to "take her love in" - and give it back.

That night, Aquarius made it up and down the stairs. The next morning, as all of us talked, I realized she had come to each of us in the night, and spent some personal time. She'd curled up beside each of us, one at a time, and let her presence, and her love, be known - even to Julian, who she saw much less often as he lived in another state. Julian remarked upon it, as her visit surprised him.

It was a soft and beautiful Christmas with Aquarius.

Two days after the boys left, Aquarius died.

When we came home from the vets without her, I went into the bathroom. And there, on the floor where I'd sat with her the night before, were two feathers. Two small, fluffy white feathers.

The bathroom had no window, and there was absolutely no way for feathers to suddenly appear here. Those many years ago, I asked myself again and again, "Could this have been a sign from Aquarius? My dear Aquarius."

Fast forward many years later, to the conference. The intelligent, gentle woman who'd shown us her "Pennies from Heaven" photo, continued by telling us how her wonderful cat had passed over and how she then found these feathers in their bathroom - a place where it was impossible for feathers to be.
      Two white feathers - exactly the same experience as my own.
      Ahhh. I felt such peace.
      Such is the beauty of our animals and their signs of love. Their soft and steadfast service to our hearts is something to behold. When Aquarius passed, she gave me a magnificent gift. She somehow stopped time and made me feel the vast Unconditional Love in Heaven, on the Other Side. Even in death, she was giving. And even now, my boys love to look at photos of their devoted Aquari.

As it was with Aquarius, so it was with my next great cat, Sadie. She was there for me, helping me survive and knit my heart back together after Allen died. Jim was home at the time, and she meant the world to both of us. And in the same way that Aquarius had tended me during my illness, Sadie settled herself in Jim's lap and tended him mightily through the worst part of his long-term illness. At times, he could only play on the computer, but she was there, perched in his arms. He still cries good tears when he looks at photos of Sadie in his arms, warming his heart, giving him comfort of all kinds.
      But Sadie's life was not as long as that of Aquarius. Our sweet Sadie died unexpectedly early, at just 4 years of age. We had tried everything to save our dear Sadie. The vet liked her so much, she came over in her SUV in the middle of the biggest snowfall I'd ever seen in all my years in the Portland area - just to get her some shots and give her acupuncture to boost her immune system. My kind vet and I were on first name basis. "Dr. Courtney" loved each animal, but tried not to get *too* attached, so she could serve them

well, but she had become very attached to Sadie. So when I took Sadie in for the final time to the vet, we *all* were emotional. Everyone knew my story with Allen, too.

That's why, after her last shot, when they left me alone in the room with Sadie, they so caringly gave me extra, uninterrupted time. I literally cried my eyes out. I cried for Sadie, and as everyone so kindly expected, I cried my eyes out for Allen. I cried and cried. I let it out. From the deepest parts of me, I let it out. These honest tears help us clear the reservoir we may not even know we had. And Sadie helped me.

I feel that, in such a beautiful way, our pets volunteer to come and spend this life with us. They volunteer to be here for us, and to steadfastly help mend our hearts.

They so beautifully volunteer. They become our feathers.

After Sadie's passing, Jim had also moved into his own place, and I suddenly felt the emptiness in my home, so I went out and bought a soft teddybear. I let myself hold it whenever I wanted to. And then in a few months, I went to my local pet rescue center, and found a white kitten (like the white in the feathers). Her kitty antics broke me out of my ruminations about Allen, and put a smile back on my face. What a giggle she was! She also helped me (and my friends) in completely unexpected ways, as you'll find out in a later chapter about Healing.

As I looked into my new kitty's bright blue eyes (bright eyes!) - even before I knew everything she would give me - I named her Bella. It means Beautiful.

As I type right now, Bella-with-the-beautiful-spirit is scampering through the kitchen-dining room area, joyfully terrorizing the artificial mouse. She's still making me laugh, and it feels good after the tears that just spilled out as I was writing about these wonderful cats.

Here's a little lightness - some of my cat-poems about these great cats.

The cat rests so hard
her head falls back, into dreams.

Yet her paw finds me.

"Twins"

Allen falls asleep
on one couch, arms above him.
New kitten falls asleep
on the other couch,
head down,
arms stretched out above her,
like a fluffy mirror of my husband.
Friendship begins
with a purr.

"Courage of the Heart"

                    The cat hopped
into the writer's dream of arms,
broke his concentration
                    like a dropped glass.
but writer knew after only brief thoughts
of a groan
                    that this surprise
                    patch of fur
had opened his heart, to leap up
so far. In split second response
                    the writer's arms hopped
up to catch his friend's
                    pure courage of heart.

Just as our cats, our dogs help us heal in a myriad of ways.
So, too, do our friends volunteer to help us, each in their own way,

during the darkest nights of our souls.   Here is a poem I wrote in honor of my grown boys and my friends who helped me when, at first, I found it hard to help myself.   Both my boys were pure champions.

"The Sherpas & the Himalayan Skies"

Jim waited. Julian waited.
My friends waited. My two sons
and my dear friends
waited for me to come back.
To come back from a long journey
into the night,
into the Himalayas,
into the place behind the stars.
After my husband's death
we all suffered.
As for me,
I took a long journey
into a hermit's place,
into the darkness of a cave
that asked to be explored -
by touch more than by sight.

But Julian waited. And Jim
waited. And my friends waited.
Knowing my spirit was not
wholly there with them,
they brought water to the opening
of the cave. Knowing my innermost
heart was busy, they sent prayers,
each in their own way.
And knowing of the pain I carried in,
they sent me thoughts of who I'd been,
but, more importantly,
they sent me messages -
messages of being loved, just for being.
For being tender now. For being vulnerable.

For being me, in whatever condition I was in.

And one day, after a seeming eternity,
as if I'd just awakened from some sleep,
I came out of the cave,
I came out of the darkness,
and I came out of the Himalayas -
but with a little piece of it in me,
and if people look closely
in these new days that I now tread,
they will see surprising sparks of light
from the place behind the stars in me,
and they will see my sons and friends
glowing inside the heart of me,
and they will see my husband,
sitting on a rock beside a stream,
chatting with me.
And they will see my Hermit's smile
as I left the cave and saw the sunlight -
knowing the people who loved me
and greeted me there, had waited,
and believed, and helped me
and even helped themselves
find our way in the darkness -
themselves becoming
astounding sparks of light,
the sparks of light who grew brighter
in times of need,
becoming true Sherpa guides,
who smile quietly in their trek,
knowing the starlit brotherhood
that shines steadfastly,
day or night,
comforting and being comforted -
creating the brilliant beauty
of the Himalayan skies.

Close family and friends play an invaluable role in our healing. And as my sons helped me, I also reached out to help them. The giver is always enriched by this process. In the giving, we also receive.

Here are some ways my family and friends helped. *I hope it will give people ideas in how to help someone who is grieving.* It's important to note that the person in mourning tumbles through a vast variety of emotions. Just as sometimes it helped for Sadie or Bella to scamper past me to chase a mouse, it also helped at other times when one of them curled up on my lap or on my chest and purred my pain away. All three of my great kitties had the same gift: they listened to my heart, then acted in accordance with what they perceived I needed that day.

If kitty-cats can do it, as friends, so can we.

At first, our friends give us the gift of tending to our hearts. Then hopefully, we will learn to do the same for ourselves. May they inspire you in both ways.

Secret Number 20:
*Tend Your Heart
by Listening to its daily needs.
Open your heart to your close family & friends,
so they can tend you, too.*

Here's a sprinkling of what my family and friends did for me.

- My friends kept in contact with me. Sometimes just a phone call is all it takes. Julian called often from Seattle, and I always felt better as I heard his concern. We could share our path of grieving together, and we could also share our lifetime of love for Allen. He had a way of bringing up concrete memories with Allen (as in his eulogy) that made us happy as we celebrated our love for a great father and husband. It was deeply consoling. Now, on Allen's birthday, or the anniversary of his passing over (his "other" birth-day in spirit), we still talk about the concrete details of our memories of Allen, of what we love about him. And it still feels good. We also actively celebrated most major holidays and birthdays together. Julian made a great effort, often traveling from Seattle to the Portland area, to make that happen.

- Jim was living with me, and he listened very beautifully. In the middle of the night, when pain decided to visit, Jim would come in and sit on a nearby whicker chair. Ever so patiently, he would listen not just to my words, but to my heart. He let me cry. He shared my tears. And eventually, he would say the wisest things that reflected the depth of what I was feeling, the pain I felt, and the love I had for Allen. The love we all had for Allen. And that continually brought me back from tears to a place of Peace. Jim was the best counselor I could have had!

- Friends took time to call and ask about me, and like E.T., they sometimes shared the experiences they'd had with their own Loved Ones on the Other Side.

- People not only sent cards of condolence, but they wrote personal notes in them. Each personal note helped us in some way.

- Some friends just hung with me. I remember my warm-hearted friend and colorful writing student, Mona. After another kind of loss, that of divorce, she told me how her new renter, a student, would just go sit on a bench with Mona. Sometimes they didn't even talk, but Mona knew someone was there for her. She was not alone, and years later, it still meant the world to her.

- My neighbor, Liz, served me soup from my kitchen. It was one of those moments when I could no longer be strong. Because of circumstances, almost all the planning for Allen's ceremony fell upon my shoulders. My sons and I were scheduled to go out and view Allen's body, and when I sat down on the couch, I found I couldn't move. I couldn't get up. There was no more in me. Just as I fell apart, Liz came over and asked what she could do. She very lovingly served us the soup. So even though we could hardly talk, we were able to drive out to say our farewells to Allen.

- Another set of neighbors put up Christmas lights for us. They did it for several years, until Jim and I figured out a way we could do it for ourselves. Every Christmas I appreciate driving up to the lights that shine so brightly in the Winter's darkness.

- People brought tons of food to our home during the day of Allen's Celebration of Life. But afterward I wish they would have done so a little while longer. Maybe people think a widow can fend for herself better than a widower, but that's not always the case during grief. Recently, one of my friends, Don, had signed up for Wheels on Meals during his wife's illness, and kept it up for a while after her death. (See the story about Dee's passing in the chapter, "Bridges.") He also continued receiving dinners from friends, which he found very helpful.

- Not one, but as I remember now, TWO people anonymously sent me beautifully knitted "Angels of Hope." I was finally able to give one of them to someone else at her time of suffering, but I still kept one for myself.

- People asked me to their events, when I was a bit better. They also drove, which is quite a relief at times of suffering.

- Bev Martin had me over to her house, and pointed out the hawk! I also had an intuitive session with Bev later. In her higher vision from Spirit, she "saw" Allen's book cover. She saw the swirl in some part of his name on the cover, and said at first he didn't know what to think as I designed it - but then he loved it. Allen said it turned out great! I then showed Bev the finished book, and we laughed our heads off. The beautiful swirl of the S in Stephens did look awesome!

- It seemed almost all of the people in Hillsboro donated funds to help me, or to help me publish Allen's Western after he had passed. I thought of them as I edited his manuscript, designed the cover, took the cover photo, and worked through all the layers publishing entails. Their support gave me wings.

- A friend from Hillsboro suggested one of the perfect songs for Allen's Celebration, "I Can Only Imagine," by MercyMe. Julian brought the other great one, "Simple Man," as mentioned. Both of these songs brought a sense of bright light we still feel. They created something good we could hold onto, and now they mean even more.

- Another friend took me shopping for Christmas ornaments, knowing this would help me through some of the bumps of the first holidays.

- Julie had just lost her father. She suggested I take some time off after Allen's death. Allen and I had just set up our publishing house two months before his passing. I thought I needed to get back to it. Because of Julie's wise advice I took one week off, then another. I needed time to process everything, from paperwork to the callings of my heart. I eventually realized the publishing house was too much for one person to handle at that time, and set it aside. I didn't put my book, "The Art of Prayer & Tea & Thee," on Amazon, but I still sold about 4,000 copies (over the years), and I did feel moved to give some inspiring Tea Ceremonies, and to publish and fulfill orders for Allen's book. I was glad Julie had taken time to speak with me, as this was a huge change for the energetic person I was - but I had been hit by the two-by-four of grief. I needed the grace - for time to heal, and for time to find my own, much gentler creative pace.

- Kathy and Jack Wood (Allen's manager at Schwan's) gave me a plant and a CD. As I cared for the plant, it imparted its life-giving energy to me, and made me realize I was still part of life. And the meditative musical CD helped me get to sleep at night - for many, many years. What gifts!

- Bruce Sussman and his lovely wife, Kelli (who were working on our website for Flowers of the Spirit), immediately put together a memorial brochure for Allen's Celebration of Life, complete with color photos. We didn't have to lift a finger! We still look at it and feel Allen's warmth - and send Bruce and Kelli a thank you.

- Connie and Paulina and their adult daughter Lisa came to the get-together at my home, even after their car had broken down at the Celebration of Life. They hugged me in the middle of the church parking lot, and said, "No problem." Still, my heart was greatly lifted when I saw these dear friends come in my front door, as if nothing had happened!

Well, you get the idea. This is a mere snapshot of the kind things people did for us. These gifts are also clues. They await our touch. As we revive, these very gifts are some of the gold nuggets that can help us come back to life - if we use them. But we are so human . . . we often forget.

"The Butterfly & Life"

Wings flutter over the river several times,
then spread to glide . . .

I keep forgetting
the second part!

As my grandmother used to say, "We have to laugh!" Because we are human, we are certainly not perfect. But the point of being here, on the Earth, is not to be perfect, but for our souls to become perfected - a bit at a time, a leap at a time, a whisper at a time. It is important to know that even when we forget, we can begin again, with love - and then begin *again* with love (see Chapter One).

At this juncture in our enlightened learning, we realize we need practice. It is time to thank our friends, Higher Spirit and our

Loved Ones. Because of all these gifts, we walk with Love in our hearts, so maybe we can take the next step - into learning the Art of Sacred Practice. Maybe we can take an active part in filling our life with more Balance and Grace. Maybe we can learn to spread our wings - and glide like the butterfly, who teaches us many things.

Chapter Twelve

The Mindful Path:
The Art of Sacred Practice

"When you find your place, practice begins."
- Dogen

When our heart breaks during the process of grieving, it can break open and become a bigger heart, if we let it. But to let it do so, we need to activate our own participation - not just the superficial movements of our bodies as we go about our daily life, but the activation and encouragement of our heart within all we do, and especially within the attitudes that direct our ship. This is a Pinnacle Decision. After the initial shocks and pains of grief, which way will we go? Will we just become a stagnant bookmark, or will we decide to add our heart and good energies to the people and the world around us?

Secret Number 21:
Choose to use Good Energy;
Decide to Add to the World around you.

The Good Path requires both Virtue and Character. As all of us know, grief can lead us to a dark place. It can take us down a rabbit hole of suffering that makes everyone around us suffer, too. During this time, we have the opportunity of becoming a permanent grouch who loses sight of everything except his or her own suffering. We can become the star of a great disaster, but this is very dangerous for our soul. That kind of thinking and behavior can draw in the negativity that is probably the opposite of what we want. Instead, we may be wanting some empathy, and some help. To do that, we will need to show our vulnerability, and we may not have been taught to do so. We also need to reach out and softly become part of the Circle of Life, each of us in our own way. And we may wonder how to do so in these altered circumstances. Each life is different, but now is the time to learn.

The path to healing requires the participation of our heart - put into practice. When we activate our own spirit to do it, it becomes The Art of Sacred Practice.

The practice is very worthwhile and pays dividends immediately. After all, it does feel good to open our hearts during grieving, and to use our vulnerability to heal, instead of using it to close our hearts and become grumpy and testy. And it does feel good to build upon the love you received from your Loved One, and bring that love forward into this life now. It feels good to base our actions on Love - both for ourselves and others - and take steps that put this Love into action.

"How wonderful it is that no one need wait a single moment before starting to improve the world."
                                                    - Anne Frank

Baby steps will help us as we begin to renew our Good Life. Sacred Practice is an exquisitely beautiful centering process. It consciously connects us in new ways to that which we love. Gently, we can build upon what we had before, and we can let our Loved Ones help us see they are part of this new life. In fact, our Loved Ones are anxious to help us with our daily lives, and to help our hearts expand into the vast new territory of *Love beyond measure.* So don't leave your Loved Ones behind in this process. Put them in your pocket, like wildflowers, and let them imbue your life and your steps with meaning, with gentleness, and with the light that will move you forward - and make them proud.

As you make small steps, you may feel small glimmers of light at first, but eventually you will become that light. You will become a beacon for others, and if you could look down from Heaven, you would be stunned at all the people you affect! One word to a stranger might brighten a day. One act of kindness might open a heart. One hug may heal someone. I think of how Julian hugs me, and I feel Allen's hugs within it. Oh my, what a wonderful gift from Julian! And I think of Jim's hugs and sweet words, and I feel healed and inspired, knowing Jim has taken my hand and is helping to lead me through life. What a kindness of the heart that is! Here are just some of his healing words:

> *Our spirits flow like leaves on the wind and sometimes the leaf that we are swirls near to the gates to the afterlife, and in those moments we sense our Loved Ones who have passed.*
> *All that you do, Mom, is a manifestation of Dad's nearness."*
>
> - Jim

Yes, when the heart is broken, it can let in more light. Jim's words call me into that light, and I try to do so by allowing Allen's love to move through me and my days in an active form. In life, we have the choice to be active or passive. Sometimes it's hard, but taking small active steps gets us there - to the place that pleases our Loved Ones greatly.

This process (known the world over by many cultures) is called a Practice, because it includes both learning, and remembering to act upon what we have learned.

"The Flash of Fireflies"

Sometimes you see
the whole panorama.
You understand in a flash.
But then it's gone,
like fireflies in Summer's
evening heat.
A flicker, then it's gone.
But that's enlightenment.
First you see it. Then
you seek it, and practice.
Practice - until
you become friends.

If our actions can be a tribute to our Loved One's nearness, then what do we want to do? And how do we want to do each thing? In the book, "Chop Wood, Carry Water," by Rick Fields, Peggy Taylor, Rex Weyler & Rick Ingrasci, we see how Love can be manifested in the way we do everyday things.

Secret Number 22:
Practice Symbolic Actions.

Center yourself, by standing in the Circle of Love
from your Loved One & Higher Spirit -
then find a way to intentionally activate
its life-giving power
in your daily life.
Small symbolic steps have great power.

As I look out upon the Japanese Cherry Tree this spring, I notice how a few blooms initially begin the process. Most assuredly, they will be followed by more, until the entire tree is a cloud of soft pink blooms. That's the way it is at first with practicing symbolic actions. Feel free to start small, with the first blooms. Even know that starting small is a smart policy. During grief, your energy level, and your desire-to-do-things level can wain, so small steps help you break through your own stuck-ness. Small symbolic steps are thankfully quite easy, but they deliver a beauty your spirit needs. These small actions will symbolize anything you want them to. Maybe they'll symbolize or honor your Loved One's presence; your love for your Loved One; or any of the things you're learning. These heart-felt, meaningful acts will give you confidence as each one lifts your spirits and makes you want to do more.

I started small. I bought a dragonfly necklace that symbolized Allen's spirit being with me. But years later, I was happy when the boys gave me another dragonfly necklace. One gift grew into another. My thoughts of staying connected with Allen in this diaphanous way were shared by others in my family - and that helped me once again. The Wheel of Healing was turning in all of us.

A funny thing happens when we start practicing symbolic actions: we start centering ourselves. As graceful as butterfly wings, it starts getting us out of our very understandable feeling of lack, into a higher place of love, and appreciation. Whenever I looked at the dragonfly necklace or any of the other dragonflies that began showing up on my shelves, I "took a step up" to meet them there. Then one day, I just had to paint one. My dragonfly painting allowed me to get to know the dragonfly spirit even better. I call it, "Beyond Boundaries." It graces the wall above the fireplace in our family room. I look at it and think about how I made the journey from feeling boxed in (in an early dream after Allen passed), to breaking through boundaries (from This Side to the Other Side, and in many other ways) - on freedom's wings.

In a multitude of ways, the Dragonfly still is working within me, teaching me and bringing me its healing messages of "no boundaries."

If you're wondering how to get this Good Energy started, know you don't have to paint to practice a symbolic action! Finding a photo, a small figurine, a postcard, a stone, a feather, or a frig magnet will do. In fact, they're great because you have room to put them where you can see them often.

Other symbolic actions can be a bit grander. I took my sons on a bold trip, not just to a nearby city, but to Hawaii. It was quite difficult at first. Getting our act together to actually get in motion was challenging as we grieved. Easier to keep our heads down and not think about things. But this is why it's called a Sacred Practice. You are putting your thoughts into action - here in reality.

As Jim said today, *"Knowledge + Experience = Knowing. And when you know something, your world is changed. You can theorize your way to Mars and back, but it is still just theory. It is like walking away from the Path. It lacks humanity because it is only our theorized concepts.*

If you are contemplating what a most noble person would do, but you don't do it, then you don't see it moving in life. We need to take Knowledge as a seed and water it with harmonious action, so we can watch it become a plant - and then we will be fed on a spiritual level."

So planning and taking this trip to Maui was like that. It worked on me, on so many different levels, and it took me out of my comfort zone. I knew it would when I did it, so part of Sacred Actions is simply knowing you're doing things for a spiritual, growth-oriented reason. When we arrived there, the boys and I had many healing conversations, because we were given the sweetness of time just to express ourselves with each other. We talked about Allen, about our grief, about our love. We shared, shoulder to shoulder, coffee cup to coffee cup - and then we swam.

We even went to a magnificent luau that lasted well into the starry night. As I looked back on my journal notes, I realized my boys danced with me - under yet *another gorgeous Full Moon!* As you can see, the trip was full of grace. And it was well worth doing, as it also kindled Bravery in us.

These ideas come from a centered place, so are done with Intention. That's why they carry a healing capacity with them. We wanted to honor Allen, and continue to build our family, and it did just that - even a bit more. Indeed, I brought back much from Hawaii - all of us did.

Sometimes you can find the keys to what symbolic actions are calling you, within the problems or challenges you face. Along our journey, we found it more difficult to celebrate our birthdays without Allen. So on Jim's birthday, we decided to break the mold. Looking to the skies, we chartered a helicopter that flew us all over the Seattle area, up and up into the sheer, snow-covered slopes of the Cascade Range. I know Allen was with us, chuckling in happiness, as his brood decided to live colorfully instead of fading away.

All these small and larger symbolic actions have a secret: they inspire you, and they change you for the better. And you find yourself looking up, and admiring yourself. You are no longer a victim; you are an active force in the Universe. You are connected, on both sides of the Veil. And in a way, *you are more Limitless than before.* Even starting out with a smidgen of a Sacred Symbolic Action will move your feet on a Higher Path.

Dr. Gordon Livingston said, *"A lot of people die with their music still inside them."* Step by symbolic step, you show how you've decided this won't be you! And in this way, when your Loved Ones check in on you, they are happy because (without ever intruding in the privacy of your life), they get to be part of the color and expression of your life, too! And as you can see, *YOU are really the painting!*

Secret # 23:
Use Noticing and Mindfulness.
Un-cloud your Mind -
to find Wisdom
and Guidance.

There is such an abundance at our fingertips, if only we look. But often during grief we practice willy-nilly actions that get us nowhere because we're not paying attention to our growth - or our thoughts. But the Higher Path requires more than that. During this time we can be very self-destructive, or very self-constructive. The quality of our life before us will depend upon our very vital choices. We'll affect ourselves, and our friends and families, and even the trajectory of our souls, so we want to live mindfully.

To do that is a remarkably easy thing to do. I think our Creator gave us some gifts that are very accessible - and attainable. As we use them, they un-cloud our mind.

"And God is able to make all grace abound toward you, that ye, always having all sufficiency in all things, may abound to every good work."
- 2 Corinthians, 9:8

In this Abundance, answers exist. But it requires us to *ask for guidance.* A fun example of this is how you can ask for a parking place when you're going somewhere. My friend, Sally, has the nickname of Rock Star because she practices this (as I do, too), and we get what we call "Rock Star Parking."

These requests also require something else. They require *an open heart that is centered upon Love.* To receive something, we need to recognize there is someone or something that gives it to us. Some people call it simply Energy, or Higher Energy, or God, or Love, or Higher Spirit, or the Great Spirit, etc. Because I teach a wide variety of people, I like to honor all the wonderful words people use for the Divine.   Basically, we are saying we don't have to do everything ourselves, that in this Divine Universe, there is help and wisdom at our disposal. I have come to believe in that power because I've seen it at work. In Sacred Practice, the more you ask, the more you receive.

The best answers come in the form of insights. A simple question, "What should I do today? - or right now?" can create a tumbling waterfall of clear answers. As you go about your day, you'll find surprising insights come in. Just a few days ago, I found myself thinking that I should call a new writer friend. I had thought it the day before, and then again, I thought it. Well, not more than 30 seconds later, who should call me? You guessed it, my new writer friend! We both laughed because we know how this works.

You can ask both pragmatic and lofty questions about anything that concerns you. To do so is to live Mindfully.

The other way this works is beautiful, too. *When something catches your eye, or starts appearing more frequently in your life, you can ask what it means. What is it trying to tell you?* In that direct way, Spirit gets the clue you are listening and you are interested. You're even saying you are open for an answer. You're Noticing. Writers are well versed in this Sacred Practice. Many of my poems are written this way, and I continually discover how much beauty and wisdom is at my fingertips. Something happened one year, and as I walked near flowers, they captured my attention in a very deep way. I started pausing and noticing, and asking and listening - then I would take a photograph, and write a poem about it. I was amazed at what the flowers had to say! The only down side was their communications were so beautiful, I found I couldn't walk through the flowers very fast anymore!

This Noticing and Mindfulness will center you and open your heart. *If you go slower, you will see more of the wiser layers of life around you, like an aura of Love that wants to tend you. And if you breathe-in the goodness of life, and breathe-out your tension and negative feelings, you will find the Breath of Life will renew you. Like a Healing Circle of letting go and letting in, you will naturally find the spiritual oxygen of renewal.*

This deep relaxation will also open your heart to Higher Love, and that is the space from which to ask good questions. The radiance and abundance you encounter here, in your Spirit Heart, will seep into your soul, and you'll always know it when you encounter it again. It will center you in a Divine Source richer than any gold.

Once you center yourself in the abundance of Love, your world and your vision expands.

As philosopher/monk, Thich Nhat Hanh writes in "Peace is Every Step":

> *"If love is in our heart, every thought, word, and deed*
> *can bring about a miracle."*

The miracle happens first within ourselves, within the confines of our heart. It compassionately heals and then expands the spiritual circumference of our heart. That opens it up to receiving, and then more and more wisdoms, insights, guidance, and miracles can pour in.

They can pour in very quickly, or take their time. But the more you bring your heart to this Sacred Practice, the more gracefully, and the more often you will receive guidance. And then life becomes full of more layers of wisdom and Love.

Secret Number 24:
Be a Bridge of Compassion.
Help someone else.

As you progress in this way with your healing, something good hits critical mass, and you feel a healthy impetus return - that is the desire to help others. When you have found more Love (because of your mindful walk with your Loved One and Spirit), then your spiritual practice expands. You can then become a Bridge to other people.

You have gained a mighty gift. In your journey through suffering, you have gained the gift of Compassion. For me, this has been one of the greatest gifts I've ever received. Of course, I had compassion before Allen's passing, but now I really feel it. At a recent healing conference, a very athletic trainer asked the speaker/healer why he was going through so many injuries. There were many answers to this, but it also encompassed a spiritual path that was unfolding. Because of these injuries, he was experiencing what it is like to be human. To *not* be perfect. And this gift of compassion was a vital component which he was meant to take back to help his clients. To do anything, we need patience. We need to practice compassion - for both ourselves and others. In many respects, that's where the healing begins.

The Sacred Practice of being a Bridge of Compassion for someone else can express itself in many aspects of our lives. We can listen - truly listen - to another person. We can use our hearts to show we care, and then, if they are ready, we may use our ability to notice Higher Spirit's gentle guidance, and share the journey together.

The impetus to serve with compassion, and to listen to Spirit's guidance while doing so, can lead to many opportunities to use our gifts and to use our hearts.

In my own life, I felt called to teach writing, and I eventually felt the call to write this book. I held it as a huge goal for years, and then recently Spirit said to do it right now, in a given period of time, because after these several months, I was going to be very busy. I am deeply touched to say that even the rough draft chapters of "The Mystery School of Grief" have been flying out the door. My son gave his copy to a friend who was sitting across from him as they had lunch. The young man was in mourning, and it was really affecting him. Jim said, "Mom, how could I *not* give it to him? It would have been like seeing someone hungry, and not giving them something to eat." So I am glad to see Spirit touch the hearts of all age groups.

Then Fran, a senior from my writing group who had just read most of the book, told me what had happened to her. As she drove through the city of Tualatin, she experienced something unusual in the midst of busy traffic. A hawk swooped right in front of her car - a Red-Tailed Hawk at that! It left her stunned.

Then shortly thereafter, the same day, she found a shiny "Penny from Heaven," and was now sputtering and giggling. "This is really too much!" Fran said with happy awe.

But as we know, it isn't. Fran had lost her dear brother, Peter, in the last several years, and these grace-filled signs of affirmation were just what she needed. As Spirit knows, it was not too much.

In all these ways, when we reach out to others, we can be a Bridge of Compassion, and Spirit's work of healing both ourselves and so many others can begin, and multiply. If we listen to what Spirit wants us to do, we start to live a wiser and more expansive life.

There are so many ways to give your heart and mind to your Sacred Practice. It could be through *Meditation and Prayer, finding Joy in the smallest of things, using energy-rich Words of Affirmation, honoring the wise gifts of wisdom Nature brings, choosing the Higher Path during each day, Dancing or Drumming or Singing, going in for Healing Sessions, learning new spiritual things, practicing your art or writing or music (etc.), and saying your Gratitudes, etc.* Thanking Spirit for everything we receive is paramount to our spiritual growth, as it both recognizes it and cements it in place, but it also does honor to Spirit, and to the multitudinous ways Spirit has given to us.

As we practice all these things, we become a Catalyst for Good. We change the energy within ourselves. We change the energy within another heart. We even change the energy within a room, as you can see when intuitive/healer, Candia Sanders, speaks at a workshop. She teaches us how to "stand in our Light." And in all these ways, as we make our Sacred Practice a central part of our lives, our good hearts - our compassionate and helpful hearts - help us enter a new dimension. We enter into the greater dimensions of Healing, both for ourselves, and for the way we can help others, each in our own way, each in our own time.

Part of our Sacred Practice is to look over the course of our life to see how Sacred Events have been woven together over time. What are the markers that lifted us into a higher level of being? What were the Belvederes that wove their way through our life and brought a larger perspective into view? What made us start to understand the spaciousness of Spirit, and the signs Spirit was there, right in our midst?

Chapter Thirteen

Touching Experiences -
From Rivers, Butterflies, Herons, Grandmothers,
Healing Hands of Light, Angels, & Dreams

It's funny, how we are when we're growing up. I'd had mystical experiences beside the banks of two mountain streams, the Salmon River and the Sandy River, both flowing from the heart of Mt. Hood. It was a powerful place. But even then, I found myself in my late 20's, wanting *a mystical experience.* I'd heard about some, and wow, I thought that would be something! Little did I think about how I was discounting all the powerful insights I had gained while naturally learning to meditate on the banks of two gorgeous rivers! *It was very mystical, in that many mysteries were unfolding and causing my spirit to be stronger.*

My parents were alcoholic then, and the woods and the sparkling rivers caught my attention and held it. I found myself casting questions up and out, into the arms of these awe-inspiring rivers. It helped me "get out" what was bothering me, and then, as I sat quietly on the riverbank amongst large sun-warmed boulders, lush ferns, dancing big-leafed maple trees and grandfather fir trees, I started feeling the beautiful response of natural wisdoms come back into my heart. Discernment can start early. I knew this was from Spirit. It taught me how to ask, and how to open my spirit to receive. And the answers helped my aching heart. The outdoor time I spent breathing in this Divine guidance proved to be an incredible, healing antidote to the chaos that thrived in my parents' house. In a sense, this time in my river-forest made me who I am today.

I wish everyone could have this environment, and these natural experiences. Later, when I went away to college in Portland, I became very happy to learn via books and tapes, how to meditate without having to be physically beside my beautiful rivers. This worked well, as I often closed my eyes and visualized myself in my magical, healing place. So this is something everyone can do. It helped me take my peaceful source along on my journey. I now carried my river-forest with me.

Years later, after earning my Art degree, I was settled in a home with a big garden, but no rivers (just in meditation time or in actual visits back to the Mt. Hood area). I remember the day well. It was in July and the morning sun was shining across our vegetable garden. I'd planted every seed and seedling, and couldn't believe the results. "What a bounty," I thought, as a serenity came over me. I really could grow things! Before I knew it, I saw a small white butterfly. It fluttered around me. And then another joined it. And another. It was a beautiful moment, and I realized it was a momentous one. As I stood still, happily surrounded by the soft wings of these white butterflies dancing around me in uplifting, ephemeral circles, I took it all in, and then I asked what it was trying to tell me.

It was then I knew a most magnificent thing . . .

It was then I knew I was pregnant!

As this profound knowing settled into me, I grinned from ear to ear, and my heart danced with the butterflies!

Later I realized that - yes! - I'd had a mystical experience. Months after my son, Jim, was born, I wrote about this mystical moment, which was such an awesome Announcement of his spirit coming into our lives:

"Short Dance"
(for my son, Jim)

before you were born
before i knew we had conceived;
before it all, one day in the garden -
butterflies danced and danced around me.

it will take me twenty years
of living with your heart in mine
to know everything
the butterflies told

Like the generous spirit of the rivers, Jim's spirit keeps on giving to me, and as you can see, the spirit of Jim's ongoing healing touch fluttered around me during my walk with grief.

Secret Number 25:
Moments Surrounding Birth & Death
Create a Magical Crack between Two Worlds,
Allowing a Glimpse into the Mysteries.

I've also come to think that in times surrounding birth and death, there is a crack between two worlds, a sacred space where one might glimpse just a little bit more of the mysteries. As I look back upon my life, another event had awakened me to think about these things. I'm fascinated at how, together, these experiences form a tapestry of Sacred Events, events which would naturally weave together to form my Sacred Practice. I'd written about this in my Sherwood Gazette newspaper column this year, "Writing - for the Life of It!"

It began with a photo I took of a beautiful Great Blue Heron at our wildlife preserve nearby. Here's a portion of the article (in which I've now added some extra details):

The heron's tall expressive legs, like matchbox fishing poles, held up a graceful body that seemed fascinated with looking at everything, with feeling everything. A brush of wind ruffled its feathers. The rain made the heron pull its feathers in, hunch its shoulders, and hunker down a bit. But *I got the feeling that even though the Great Blue Heron was alone, per se, it didn't feel alone. The Mallard Ducks, the rain, the log, the air, the mist - they were all a part of it.*

Within this beautiful picture of a stately animal that met rain with grace, and didn't turn to hide or fly away, was the bonus of a mirror reflection of the Great Blue Heron, as it stood by a pond and took in time, as if changing it by loving every moment of time. The mirror reflection made me think of two worlds, of this world and of the Other Side, so close they touch and have the capacity to expand us, even if we've never thought of the mystery of Life and Death before. I think of another time, lo many years before, when I was a young college woman and my date's grandmother approached death. She'd been to the hospital before, but had come back home. It hadn't been her time, she told us . . . but now it was. I was in the middle of a date with her adult grandson, Dan, when it happened.

"When? . . . Now???" The words flew through my head like fastballs over the home plate of a baseball diamond. What had started out as a date suddenly turned so serious that time stopped to let the huge scope of everything in.

"She's asking for you," Dan and his mother said, motioning to the bedroom door. In an amazing turn of events, this older woman I had barely met was a wise woman who was ever so kindly leading us all through a portal I'd never been near before. She had something to say to each one of us, so she kindly met with each of us privately. It struck me how she knew she was departing. And it also struck me how full of grace she was. Like the Great Blue Heron, she was part of this world and the reflection of the next, at the same time.

I couldn't tell you what she said to me, but she introduced me to death as a passing over, as a passage. As a sacred rite. One hour later, she died. But she had closed many of the doors of fear for me, and opened up the doors of mystery.

Then decades later, when Allen's mother, Evelyn, had congestive heart failure, I held her hand quite steadily, at the same time that my words spoke like an alarm bell, "Call for an ambulance - NOW!" I knew every second counted, for as I held her hand, I could feel her spirit leaving . . . leaving. It was leaving fast now. It was almost on the Other Side! . . . and then ever so slowly, her spirit started to come back.

We were blessed to have Evelyn for some months after that, but the night before she eventually passed over, she could no longer talk. I noticed she was looking at something at the end of her bed, but no one was there. After we wished her good night, and started walking down the hallway, I told Allen I had to return to say something else to his mom. I gently took her hand and told her I loved her, and then I asked her what she had been looking at. "Were those Angels at the end of your bed?" Her eyes instantly brightened with happy surprise, and for one dear, priceless moment, she regained her voice and managed her last beautiful word. Clear as a bell, she said, "Yes!" And so it was that years later, I think of this again. After facing the death of Loved Ones, I am now like the heron, in love with Life and with the reflection that captures both worlds at once.

In so many ways, we can feel alone in this world of Life and Death. But I have been lovingly taught. There are so many reasons to know we are not alone. To know that love on both sides of the Veil is a very big thing. The Great Blue Heron knows this. I know this. And when you do, Life hands more of its gifts to you.

Two major things happened when, at first, Evelyn almost passed over. Through my hands, I felt the tremendous, beautiful energy of her spirit blending with Higher Spirit as her spirit was leaving. She made it to a doorway, a threshold of some kind, and then paused, and came back. Probably was sent back. It seems she had more to do.

Also, later she told me how, in the hospital that night, she had seen her ex-husband. Only her ex-husband was on the Other Side! His eternal spirit, which was much healed, was there to meet her, and he extended his hand, ready to help her over to the Other Side.

This was stunning, because they'd definitely not gotten along during their years of marriage, early in her life. Obviously, he'd learned a lot on the Other Side!

Looking back, I see how Spirit had given her longer to live, because after she had almost passed over, she then took time to contact all her children, including a step-son in California I didn't even know about. Amends were made, and peace was found. He has since passed over, so I more deeply understand Spirit's timetable.

As I now start thinking about the vital energy that began coming through my own hands when I held Evelyn's hands, and then later, through Reiki hands of Light healing, I think back to an even earlier memory. In church when I was young, I remember the same light-filled energy entering my hands. The energy was warm, and vibrated like electricity through my hands and through my fingertips, as if wanting to be expressed. These quiet moments of prayer-time were my favorite moments in church because of this, and because of the prayerful, meditative state I was in. Later, I would think of this warm, life-giving energy in my hands as part of my gift of writing. It directed me to write from a wise and healing place. But this energy also expanded at a time I least expected it - not when I was energetic and able, but when I was suffering from the illness we couldn't cure yet.

Secret Number 26:
Spirit's Healing Energy has a POWER to it.
Let yourself feel it!
Ask it to come in.

As I've mentioned, so many years later, I was dramatically sick from the toxic overload in my body, but one particular day while I was meditating, a radiant energy suddenly flowed through my body. Its power coursed through me and went in an entire oval circuit around my body. I was listening to a healing CD, and opened my eyes, wondering if I'd fallen asleep. Surely, this wasn't real. The powerful energy then immediately zapped around the entire oval circuit of my body again - like lightning! - as if showing me I wasn't sleeping or imagining things!

This incredible experience was a lifetime Wower - and caused my healing to take a huge leap.

Not long after that, I had more hard-to-explain Sacred Experiences when I went to a top-notch healer visiting from England. It was my first visit to a healer, but I wasn't going for myself. It was for a friend who was really bad off. The person could hardly talk. I took a deep breath, and hoped for the best. The healer startled me by saying we had to change around the flow of this person's energy! "Wow, can that be done?" I must have uttered.

But, since I'd had my "Circuit of Lightning" experience, I thought, "Maybe we could do this." The kind, sensitive healer showed me how to gently put my hands on my friend's forearms - then to feel the flow of the energy - and then to ask that energy to flow the opposite way. And then to imagine it doing so.

This was all a *huge* step for me, but my Guidance told me to do it, and somehow I think the healer knew I was ready to do this. So I surrendered to the Divine, and as I did it, I felt the flow of energy in my friend's arms. Then, much like in Evelyn's hands years later, I felt the energy pause, adjust, and slowly start to flow the other direction! What a feeling!

As my friend's energy first began flowing in the right direction, it met blocks. I felt my friend's huge emotional blocks. As I concentrated on the energy flow and felt the blocks, I was unexpectedly brought to tears. The healer, too, was concentrating, as he was doing some energy work on my friend's back, but he sensed my questions. In awe of the power of what was happening, I opened my eyes and looked up at the healer.

He simply said, "You're doing the right thing. Keep going!"

As I did, I cried not my own tears but the tears of my friend, and my friend's energy flow strengthened . . . Finally, we knew it was time to stop. The English healer gave my friend the tiniest amount of a homeopathic remedy, and that was the beginning of this person's tremendous healing! I feel it literally saved my friend's life. It was Spirit doing the work. The healer and I just followed directions and became the conduit of Spirit's powerful energy and Love.

As I look back now, I can see how this rather incredible set of experiences opened me up to new levels of energy work. I didn't really know what energy work was, but, in Spirit's indubitable fashion, I was doing it! So it happened that a while after Allen had passed over, a friend asked me if I would like to go through a Reiki training to become a Level I Reiki Practitioner. Reiki is a hands of light healing method, begun in Japan and practiced worldwide, even by many nurses in hospitals.

While proceeding through this life-enhancing training, all my previous Sacred Experiences came into play. All the times I spent naturally quieting my mind and meditating upon Divine Spirit's Love formed an energy that wanted to course through my body, and be used for healing of all kinds. I especially like the idea of emotional healing, as it affects so many things.

As we went through our Reiki training sessions, we all worked on each other. I found that as I closed my eyes, a series of pictures would pop up - a different one for each person. Sometimes it would be a picture, or a moving picture, like a small bit of a movie. But it was meant for that person. Once again, I felt shy, but I surrendered to the innocence of working with the Divine, and shared what I was seeing.

The people I worked with found the pictures to be both meaningful and "right on!" One person had the problem of hurrying too much through life, and her image was a freight train speeding down the track. For a busy mom, this image was a helpful symbol of what she was doing, and what she wanted to change!

From there, I started doing Reiki for friends and family. It's not a business to me, but a blessing - a blessing I want to share. Often, instead of placing my hand in the given areas around different parts of a person's body in the pre-specified order, Spirit told me, "Place your hand here. Now move it there." I made an executive decision to listen to Spirit instead of only following prescribed guidelines. Recently, another Reiki practitioner told me she did it the same way, as I did, and added how many practitioners do also. Ah, I love the guidance from Spirit. Everything I was taught was invaluable, and blending it with the further Inspired Guidance I was receiving celebrates the spirit of Reiki, and the depths to which it can move powerful healing energies through hands that listen and learn.

In the last 3-4 years, I've had plenty of practice. So as I helped a different friend in a Reiki session one day, I was directed to put my hand on his leg, and Spirit's energy came through my hands. It is not my energy, but Spirit's. I'm just the conduit. All I do is open up my heart, and get my ego (and my preconceived thoughts) out of the way. As people who meditate or pray understand, that is sometimes a challenge! But the practice of Reiki (and other Sacred Practices) will help you. The more often you do it, the more naturally it comes. Soon, you can center yourself very quickly. Often, you can center yourself in a split second.

Secret Number 27:
Tears are Emotionally Healing,
but Tears are also Physically Healing.

To release that which is blocking us is so helpful, and so healing. We soon realize how much better we feel when we release our pain and sorrows as our tears fall, instead of holding them in with a tight, tense grip. I was also fascinated to learn in some healing-from-grief video I saw along the way, that tears are also *physically* healing. As I think about what I'd learned in Reiki, I feel it's because of how the healing energy flows through our body, and the blocks in our systems are acknowledged, given love - and then cleared in a natural timetable only the body knows. This allows our body to be tended and refreshed on a very deep, nonverbal level.

Letting the warm, golden light of Higher Spirit's Love come through your hands during Reiki teaches you about how we hold our pain, fears, and sorrows in our body, because Spirit concentrates on those areas. Spirit guides the placement of my hands. Some people, like Suzanne, feel the heat in my hands, and some people don't. It varies. It is nice but it doesn't matter if they feel the heat or not. Reiki works either way. I've learned to listen to a wide variety of things the body will bring up for healing. A variety of strong emotions are held in our bodies, sometimes in the form of tears. They can come out at surprising times, such as when I suddenly felt an avalanche of tears break through for myself on the second Christmas after Allen's passing.

As Jim says, he *"is glad a soul can be limber enough to have tears. With grief, you stiffen up. Your body recoils and you create a shield or block. If you don't look at it, you will lose your inner flexibility, and then, if you want to try to move, you hit a wall."*

I am often surprised by what happens in a Reiki, hands of healing light session. In this case, Spirit directed me to move my hand and let Spirit's energy flow into my friend's heart, so I did. Immediately, feelings of emotional pain came in. They were about the war in Vietnam, and they shook through his body with the force of a freight train. (Here's that freight train again!)

As when Winter's frozen lands give way to the warmer expressions of Spring, a log-jam was released, and tears began to weave their way down *my* cheeks (not his). In this beautiful place, you know they are not your own tears, but the sacred tears of the person before you. And you know in a heartbeat this person is part of your Hoop, a group of people you are connected to spiritually. Through Reiki, I have felt the tears of Vietnam War Veterans shake through me; the tears of those afraid to open their hearts to love; of those who feared walking through loss; and of those who, like all of us, felt hurt, discouraged, or stuck.

With the release of this painfully blocked emotional energy, I felt this fine, caring man's tears. Whole oceans of them! And as I felt them also move through my heart, I realized I was crying the tears he couldn't cry. As in one of my previous healing experiences I've shared with you, with Spirit's help, I was crying his tears for him!

That's what Spirit does. Spirit cries the tears we cannot cry! It does so for us!

I was only Spirit's helper. It was Spirit crying the tears my friend could not cry. In this way, Spirit was teaching me a Double Blessing. Allowing me to *feel* a Double Blessing. The magnitude of what I felt in these moments was huge. It made *me* cry more tears - tears of gratitude!

My tears for him were healing tears, and, as I've explained earlier, they continue to heal after they fall, so I didn't wipe them away for a while. Also, in a tape I heard about healing from grief, it was reiterated that *tears are physically healing.* I believe it!

I was deeply moved by this experience, so I wrote this poem for all of us. When I read it, I feel a potency in it, as it holds healings that are exquisitely personal for each of us. Please feel free to make a copy of it and use it with anyone, including yourself, and just change it from "him" to "her" or "me". This is the Forcefield of Love I felt in the session with my friend, as Angels helped both my friend and myself.

Imagine this shower of Angels. I feel they especially like songs and poems of invocation, such as this one. It invites them in simply by recognizing they are there, and opening our hearts to understand the ever-present majesty of their realm.

"The Healing Poem"

*A shower of Angels
stood around him.
Like a bright Galaxy
of shimmering Stars,
the Force of Angels
shone their warm Love
upon him,
until he woke up
in their arms.*

This healing energy has the power of Love in it, and is constantly teaching me.

Secret Number 28:
*The Double Blessing:
As Spirit flows through us,
and our Loved Ones,
we all can work in tandem
to create a bigger Circle of Healing.*

Spirit guides us in ways so spacious, it's hard to imagine at times. I felt that spaciousness as the continued warm, healing energy I'd been feeling came in during a dream in which Allen appeared.

"The Healing Circle"

I was part of a group standing in an irregular cluster. Allen's spirit helped bring refreshing, healing energy not only to me, but to all of us. Where at first we were standing at random, we then became a circle, and a circuit of energy was healing and blessing all of us. On the Other Side, Allen worked in tandem with Higher Spirit to create this Circle, and as the great healing energy passed through Allen and through me and through those around me, Love was multiplied exponentially. It was a beautiful sight.

So even as we learn to work with Divine Spirit's healing energy here on the Earth plane, so too, can our Loved Ones be working in tandem with Higher Spirit - from the Other Side! In the same way I receive healing energy from Higher Spirit during Reiki, so, too, can our Loved Ones also receive and be a conduit for Higher Spirit's loving force - conveying it to us within our dreams and our daily lives. Spirit is ever working with us!

(Another synchronistic event just happened. As I turn on the TV to take a break, a talk show comes on and immediately someone is talking about a "Prayer Circle!" Fun! That's what we could call this last dream.)

This natural way of "being there for Spirit" - by allowing Spirit's great, loving, golden energy to pass through our hands - struck me as a very positive thing to do in my life, especially since it was relaxing people's bodies/minds and spirits so their hearts could receive whatever it was Spirit wanted to send their way.

It also had the bonus of giving me insights that astounded me. I seemed to be even more aware of the Angels surrounding me, helping me in different ways. They helped me during Reiki, and they helped me with my own daily needs. But the Angels still surprised me at a time I needed them most. When my mom was dying in the hospital, the Angels used their awesome power to build a beautiful, strong Forcefield of loving protection and peace around me - one like I'd never felt before. They created something that looked akin to the two lines of football players you see when the quarterback runs through them. The Angels appeared tall, with white feathers - what can I say? That's how they felt, too. They had the amazing strength and Love Force of Archangel Michael.

They protected me with this veritable Forcefield of Grace for a week, until my mom passed over. I walked through these two beautiful rows of Angels every day in the hospital corridor immediately outside my mom's room. The shield of their Love was palpable to me. Right before she passed over, this shield started to purposely fade, and I knew it was time for me to go. I asked my mom's spirit to please pass over in these last moments I was here, if it was in agreement with her spirit. A private moment to be alone with her immediately opened up, and I walked in and took my mother's hand. She had not opened her eyes for some time, but her eyelids flickered, and then opened one last time. She smiled that mother's smile into my eyes, and I told her how very much I loved her. She squeezed my hand and we shared our own world of mother-daughter love - and then she closed her eyes and her breathing began to stop, and she passed over soon. The Angels had worked so hard on our behalf. I felt their touch in everything.

I had also felt Allen's spirit within all of this. I was protected and guided by a Forcefield of Double Blessings every "grace-full" step of the way. I was grateful beyond measure. Those days and those moments with my mom meant the world to me. I was glad I had learned Hands of Light Healing, as that, and other kinds of our Sacred Practice will bring more of these priceless moments to us as we accept the good energy that will light our way.

I want to once again say, "Thank you, Mom."

I also want to add that very often our Loved Ones wait until we go out of the room before they pass over. Hospice volunteers report this frequently. After all, the process of passing over is a sacred rite, and many things are going on during the passage. In addition to that, our Loved Ones sometimes have great difficulty saying Good-bye to us. Both Suzanne and I weren't able to say Good-bye to our husbands, but as I talked to Suzanne about it one day, I realized they never wanted to say Good-bye . . . so Leroy passed when Suzanne was out of the room, and Allen passed in an accident when he was at work. Whether we are holding their hands or we are not by our Loved One's side, there is no easy way to say Good-bye.

But fortunately, they keep coming to visit and tend to us whether we see them visually or not. This leads me to share something I learned over the years. When I was alone at night, I started feeling something sit on the foot of my bed. I thought it was my kitty-cat. But as I began to look, it often wasn't! It was then I began to listen and sense who was visiting. Allen visited many times, and just sat there and protectively, lovingly looked over me. Also, some other Loved Ones from several friends came and gave me a few messages to pass on to them. Over the years, through interesting conversations, I have come to find out from many other widows and widowers that they experienced the same thing! Who knows these things until you experience them?!

Double Blessings sometimes happen in unexpected ways. Not very long after I started doing Reiki, I received a soft surprise which I have promised to tell you about. As I practiced Reiki, I closed my eyes and centered myself, and soon the images or visions came quicker and quicker. I wouldn't think of anything; they would just happen. They were also happening to my friend who had suggested the training, only they happened to her at other times, not during Reiki. (All times are fantastic!) One day, as I closed my eyes, and started to let in the warm energy during Reiki, I almost opened my eyes in astonishment! But I kept them closed - because what I saw was so beautiful of spirit. The image I very clearly saw was of my cat, Bella - my dear sweet Bella! With her bright blue eyes, she let me know she was there. Remember, she is living with me now (not passed over) but how could I know: she was a Reiki cat! And, truth be known, she is probably more the Master of Reiki than I'll ever be!

She'll show herself in different ways. Like Allen in his "Puzzle Pieces Visitation," she'll show me just a portion of herself. Just her face and those brilliant blue healing eyes. Sometimes she'll be turned this way, or another way, and she will also blink her eyes slowly at times. In an intuitive way, I understand all of this. She's a remarkable cat. One of her messages is *"healing is occurring."* When I see her during Reiki, it is a sign that I am in the Zone, allowing Spirit to do the work. I am very thankful for Bella! But don't get me wrong, Bella also acts like a regular cat! She's rather hilarious at times.

All of these Sacred Experiences weave together in their own unique ways for all of us. Most of us have experienced at least one Sacred Experience, and many people have experienced more, even an abundance. For all of us, this is a worthy goal, to experience this beauty, and to be part of the healing it brings not only to us, but, as Allen's spirit would say, "To a greater Circle!" One way of doing this is to say our Gratitudes. It takes it to another level of appreciation, to list these Sacred Experiences, and see, as the Australian aborigines had told me in a dream: how they are woven together to form our new dreams.

Speaking of dreams, this is what came next. For some reason, I was worried about my health (if I possibly suddenly had cancer?), and I received this dream:

"The Most Wonderful Healing Dream:
The New Vibrant Green Leaf"

(In my dream): *I feel Allen, Jim and another person around. I feel I disagree with this other person who is talking about "fading, feeling less love as we age now." So I go another way.*

Then I'm in something like a treehouse, but real, spacious rooms, etc. A house.

Bev (the intuitive and friend who helped me see a Red-Tailed Hawk at her house right after Allen passed over), is opening a beautiful book, like an ancient bible with colorful art designs on the borders and the first letters of words that start the pages. Gold filigree. And it is on someone else's lap, but I am appreciating it.

Then I am over here, in my own space, as people get ready for the meeting and the healer to come.

I then see a vibrant bright green color flowing into my body - my mid-section. It is the bright green of a NEW LEAF! It is alive with life. It is like a band of living vibrant green - and it gently moves into all the places needed - gentle, beautiful, thorough.

Life! . . . Love!

I realize I am being healed . . .

Once it is complete, it turns a beautiful bright yellow - and then radiates into white - which I understand means I "should share this with others."

As this happens, I realize the healer has asked me to sit there and let this happen before. I join him in another room . . .

That room seemed to be one focused on learning more about healing. As I think about this dream, I realize - ahh - *my mom* had cancer in her mid-section before she died . . . This dream also catapulted me into a renewed commitment to my life. I then had a most wonderful dream about men, in which Allen appeared.

"My Men"

I was being helped by many men in my Soul Circle (your Soul Circle is made up of people you intuitively know are lovingly connected to you; they are a part of you and care for you on a spiritual level throughout time). One wonderful man whom I recognized joined me in working with putting both my words and my art together. We painted together, so happily, and then we combined beautiful calligraphy, Native American wisdoms (I'm part Cherokee), and poetic insights on graceful paper scrolls. He then pulled out a rough sketch of mine, and admired it. I said, "Don't use that. It isn't a finished work."

He looked into my eyes and said, "I love being part of your New Beginnings."

Then another man appeared, and Allen was not jealous. Instead, the man, Allen, and my other men decided to build some beautiful Grecian columns for me - together. As they were laying on these stones, they were all helping each other - to help me. One would give it to Allen, who was at the top (of course!), and they were all using their craftsmanship, but they were laughing together like chums. If something fell apart, they just laughed and started over again. I had a whole team behind me, helping me "build" my New Beginnings.

You never know what kind of help you're going to get from the Other Side! This dream, the healing New Green Leaf dream, and the many Sacred Experiences were helping me live my life in real time - more lightly now. Allen was helping me do this, and I was receiving things that gently thrust me into the midst of life and the people around me. Even dating. It also increased my creativity, and helped me once again to focus on putting love into everything I shared.

All these different Sacred Experiences create a beautiful tapestry. It's an interesting kind of Life Review. Looked at *before* we pass over, it is something well worth doing. By reviewing our unique Path of Sacred Practices, and how they lead us into the Sacred Experiences, we see how they open us, like a book of grand proportions. And we feel how our life is touched by the gold filigree of Spirit's fine Love. We see what weaves us together, in a good way, into our true selves - *with* a sense of humor, too! And we see all the people, including our Loved Ones on the Other Side, who bring us Double Blessings as we recognize them, and accept the offer of letting their healing Love flow into our lives.

I'm thinking about the next events I want to share. The people who are destined to help us are sometimes people we know, and are sometimes special people who come, like angels, into our path at just the right time, holding gifts of great healing that affect more than ourselves. In fact, it can affect those on both sides of the Veil . . .

Chapter Fourteen

Reconnections -
of the Boldest Kind

Renee Madsen was one of those unexpected "angels" in my life. But to give you a perspective, I need to look back for a moment and tell you more about my early life. It was a rocky life growing up with my parents. From the time I was about 12, they drank too much, and chaos reigned in our household. I knew Dad had suffered in France in WW II, and I'm sure he brought those scars back with him, just as the vets from recent wars have come back, suffering silently from PTSD. Like a host of others at the time, Mom and Dad started a family right away. They soon had four children, and probably plenty of stress. I don't blame them; I just knew it was hard on us children. There would be some moments of fun and delight, but quite often it was terrible - and scary, even after they finally stopped drinking. I had a harder time with my dad, but my mom enabled him, and that brought about another set of dramas. Despite this, I knew both my parents loved me, even as their suffering spread out into the sphere of their children.

Secret Number 29:
When Dreams of Guidance come,
your understanding of them may come later.
Track Dreams of Guidance by writing them down.

About a year after Allen's passing, I had a series of dreams about my parents, who had never been in my dreams before. They were definitely dreams of guidance, and they helped prepare my heart.

"The Mother's Blouse"

In the first dream, my mom invited me to share tea with her at the kitchen table, as we had so many times before. She said, "I have a gift for you." Beaming, she gave me her "mother's blouse." The fabric was floral and I loved it. "You are a good mother. I am handing down this Mother's Blouse to you. You deserve it." Her smile was warm and full of the mother's love I had so often felt, especially when we had time alone. But then the dream proceeded to show me my mom was going to pass over.

And in about a month, she did.

The next dream, almost a year after my mom's passing, forecast my dad's passing over, and he passed over within about a month.

It had been a tough existence for me with my parents, and my story ("Home at Last"), about finding your voice when you are in stressful situations, can be read in Kay Allenbaugh's book, "Chocolate for a Woman's Courage." Before that, a healer had also told me about my Life Purpose. I was shocked as she conveyed that it was "Truth: to Speak your Truth."

"Darn!" I'd said, maybe worded more strongly than that. With my parents problems, life was often like a battlefield with shrapnel flying everywhere. You had to hide not to get hurt. The last thing I wanted was to speak Truth to what I saw as power. But over time, I learned to set boundaries and have a voice, however uncomfortable that was. And what I thought of as power changed. I had forgiven my parents and relied on Spirit to bring a powerful kind of peace into me.

The next dream, which I received after they had passed over to the Other Side, was a short one.

"Because"

Both my parents were in work shirts. Mom and Dad were taking classes - because they loved me.

It's awesome to know learning continues, and Spirit's plan keeps unfolding as people grow. When I'd wonder about my parents, God would tell me they were busy, Mom was being comforted and was healing, and Dad was in "Basic Training!" That would make me laugh, and it also rang true.

"Just keep living your life. The time will come," Spirit added.

In the next dream, the messages from them continue.

"Learning"

I'm in a place with my mom and it's full of junk. We're stepping over it. I say, "Mom, you need to de-clutter."

But Mom and I are spending girlfriend time together. There is such love between us.

Then I see her reading a book, given to her by a young woman, and she was learning again.

What amazing dreams to have! They helped open my heart to many new potentials with my parents. Spirit showed me the book was given by me. I also was shown that our prayers for the people on the Other Side are very important, and somehow add to their healing and growth. *I've also received this message pertaining to people who commit suicide. Our prayers for them help form a bridge of love and learning. Spirit says we, too, learn by doing this for them - and for all who suffer. I think Spirit loves our participation, and so creates these opportunities to work in tandem. Yes, Spirit could do it alone, but that's not the point. Spirit wants us to grow, and so offers different ways to work with Spirit or co-create with Spirit - to advance our souls. Experience is a great teacher, and puts concepts into practice.*

When we help or pray for someone who is suffering, we come to understand we all have many beautiful things to Learn. In the process, all of us can be "reading a book."

As our spirit expands during our journey of healing during grief, we have all kinds of new experiences. And we explore things we might never have looked into before. As I was talking about such things with my dear friends, Dee and Don, they gave me the name of a well thought of intuitive, Renee Madsen, who frequently appears on a popular local TV show in Portland, AM-NW. I was pleased to get the personal referral to Renee, and as we shared, I gave them Candia's name, too. We both had sessions with each others' favorite intuitive, and we were all very pleased. We all knew we had found the best because of the incredibly accurate things that came through.

Several months earlier, I attended a meditation workshop by Renee. Afterward, I asked a question. She said, "By the way, do you know you have a lot of Angels around you? I mean, a lot!" Other than that, she didn't know anything about me until the day of my session with her. I thought about her comment, and I believe the Angels cluster around us more clearly when we listen to them. In my session, I felt many Angels cluster around both of us. Like Candia, Renee is a gentle, sweet, loving person, who lets Higher Spirit direct traffic. She very gracefully let it roll, as you will see. I didn't have a lot of expectations, other than, since I was starting to date again, I thought Renee might have some insights.

But the first person who showed up - immediately - was, of all people, my dad, from the Other Side! We'd just begun, and I was shocked when my dad came in at all, much less so quickly. He was humble and sincere. He told me how he was learning so much from the way I was living my life. That my life was affecting him tremendously.

And to add to that, his spirit came in apologizing for what he had done. For the way he had treated me. Renee conveyed the very words he was speaking, and at one point, he was having trouble talking, because of his shame. It was very edifying to see someone so full of shame they couldn't progress, and so I helped him, and told him sincerely that I forgave him - and we could start over again, right now.

With that, the energy immediately shifted. He then continued on, opening up, and really showing his heart to me, and it was very beautiful! Renee said that (like so many people) I had come in so bright when I was born, my parents didn't know how to help me. They loved me, but with all the problems my mom and dad were dealing with, they had felt bad, but they didn't have the skills to encourage me and help me grow. And they were so sorry!

With the way he had grown on the Other Side, Dad showed me how he now wanted to help me with my business (as he'd had a business during his life here), and how he had good energy now that would help me in different speaking situations, etc. How happy it made me!

Then Mom came in! I was doubly surprised! She also stressed how much she was affected by watching my life. (In this way, she HAD read the book I had brought her, as in the dream I had!) They both talked about it a lot and they both apologized, and she showed me her big time love for me.

But they also talked about the way she had run hot and cold with me emotionally, and how she was healthy now. She was a bit humbled by it.

Then Allen popped in! He said, "Yep! There are no neuroses here!" And then everyone laughed. That opened up the energy!

I haven't included everything here, but you get the idea. It is incredible to me that such healing goes on, and that Renee could bring me this gift of Reconnection - of the boldest kind. It was truly astonishing.

It has informed me every day since then.

And because of this, since then I have connected with them, and they have been there for me, softening my days with their ever-present love and support.

A few days after my session with my parents, I saw a Folger's coffee delivery truck, the kind my dad used to drive before he had his own business. At the same moment, a song came on the radio, as if sent by my dad. "The Reason" by the group, Hoobastank, spoke about not being perfect, but changing because of someone you love. For someone you love. I hope you will look it up and listen to it.

The timing was perfect, and I watched and listened quietly as the coffee delivery truck drove off, leaving me feeling I had received a Special Delivery. I thanked God for the boundless Love that is brought to us, in all kinds of seemingly implausible ways. Thank you, also, to my dear parents, who are there for me in these astonishing ways.

What a gift they gave to me by showing up in my session with Renee. *Such is the power of Love, to help all of us heal into new Love.*

Chapter Fifteen

Bridges, Drumming, & Dee

The next thing I was drawn to learn was Native American drumming. The idea, and the request from Spirit to do so came up in a Reiki session with a friend I was dating, and together we went to the Cedar Mountain Drums shop, which Candia had told us about when we wanted to know how in the world we could find a drum. We met the owner, Patrick, who talks about how they put prayers into the making of each drum. We found ones that harmonized with our hearts.

My Cherokee heritage blended with my friend's bold expressiveness, and soon we were drumming and even chanting. My friend started the chanting, as if he'd done it all his life, and I was stunned. A bit shyer, I had to ask Spirit to help me, and then soon I found my voice (again!), and had my own softer way of chanting. I like drumming and the sound of natural chanting because they are so easy, and feel so eternal. Over time, you play around a bit, and find your way to your own sound. Your own prayer. I soon understood from Spirit that each drum-song is a prayer. How beautiful is that?! As always, if you let Spirit come through you, it works more gracefully, and you learn to let your fears, your feeling of shyness, and your ego get out of your own way. Then it's a bit like Reiki. It takes you to another level. So you begin by centering yourself in the Centerpoint of Peace, and Love, and let the Divine spirit of healing and guidance enter in. Then the drumbeats enter into your heart, and together they form a Divine Instrument.

Secret Number 30:
There is a Centerpoint of Peace and Love.
You can find it.
It is where everything sacred begins.

Even as Dee and Don, Sally, Fran, John, Jim and others joined in for these playfully insightful drumming sessions, I had no idea the good places it would lead me. As I closed my eyes and drummed, new images came in, and they were very healing and insightful. It was a beautiful way to connect with Spirit.

Dee was very sick at the time, so she liked to listen quietly, taking it in, to some deep part of her soul that thirsted for it. In her fragile state, she went on her own journey, and "got" something just for her. She would smile and her eyes were full of peace afterward. Her husband, Don was there, too, "giving this new thing a go." He was shy and tentative, but he'd always wanted to do this, and he loved dipping his toes into this new world of drumming.

Native American drums don't demand complex rhythms, and there is no song sheet, thank goodness. Plus you don't have to be a singer, which I've proven! The process is so simple: you just follow along, and see where it goes. I find that so refreshing, and liberating. As we begin to play our drums, we relax, and we often close our eyes, into the rhythms of the Dreamworld. You can also do this on your own, no group needed.

This was an experience Spirit must have wanted us to have, as it opened the way for one of the most beautiful Sacred Experiences I've ever had. This happened just months ago, right before Dee passed over. After I wrote up this experience into story form, I shared it with Don, and he and his family also asked me to read it at Dee's Celebration of Life:

"The Bridge"

Taking a deep breath, I knocked softly and quietly opened the door to Dee and Don's home without waiting. "Can you handle being here as Mom passes over?" Dee's daughter, Sunny, had kindly asked on the phone just an hour ago. "There's no judgment if you can't. Some people just can't handle it." I could hear her take a deep, sustaining breath. "It's tough."

I had seen my own mom pass over in the same way, with lungs filling with fluid. We were all grateful for the pain killers that eased her passage. "I can do it," I answered, knowing also just what sacred moments these were. As soon as I entered the living room with the big hospital bed dominating it like an ocean liner, I was grateful once again that I'd been seeing Dee and sharing important conversations on an ongoing basis during this time, because now Dee was silent - her song-like voice busy in another land, her expressive eyes now closed to our conscious world.

Yet she was still here, and if she was still here, I figured there was a reason. Probably many reasons, both seen and unseen. And so I sought to enter her unseen world. As kind nurses, social workers, and even a harpist finished their tender work beside Sunny and Don, I wondered how or even IF to fit in. Their work was vital, and the buzz in the room was respectfully quiet but intense.

Soon the wonderful staff of nurses who had become instant friends had helped Sunny turn Dee on her side, and had thankfully eased her breathing. The harpist's gentle chords had settled all of us down, including me. As the many helpers talked intently with Don and Sunny about all their responsibilities, I asked permission and walked quietly to get my drum out of its purple case. Where would I play it? How would I play it and sing in a chant-like way with all these strangers around me? Suddenly I was shy, but step-by-step I was drawn to Dee's side at the top of her bed.

I had placed my hand on her shoulder just beforehand, and had felt the energy of Love's spirit connect with Dee's spirit. Silently I heard Dee's message. She told me she was half-way over The Bridge! Closing my eyes, I saw Dee light and free. Yes, it was time to drum. She wanted me to help drum her over the Bridge. To be with her during her passage. And so it was that this gave me the courage to get beyond my fears and my shyness, and to partake in a sacred journey. I played very simply, and very softly. Like a gentle whisper, a drum beat of Love. Ever so gently, I felt the drum harmonizing with her spirit.

Closing my eyes, I entered Dee's journey. Almost giddy, Dee said, "I didn't know it would be THIS wonderful." She gave me a big grin. "Oh my, this is great! The Love is incredible. So warm. So limitless. I'm surrounded by it!" She showed me the warm golden glow that expanded, and then expanded ever more. Even though we all knew Dee had lasted as long as she could and did not want to leave her loved ones, we all knew this was indeed Dee's time. It was only now that she could turn toward it fully. In this quiet, she was finally embracing her journey. Her happiness was so great, she actually made me laugh! Here I was drumming, and crying, and then laughing at the same time - all with my eyes closed. I could feel the tears stream down my cheeks. I left them there and just kept on drumming. In healing circles, it is said that these tears should not be wiped away, for they are healing you then.

As the shyness lifted, I felt my voice begin to sing - softly, and as gentle as Dee's spirit. I listened deeply, and took directions from Spirit. Eventually I realized it was Dee's song. Her very own Song of Passage. When I thought, "Oh, maybe this chant is too repetitive," Dee would tell me "I love it that way - repetitive. Don't change a thing!"

As Dee made progress on the Bridge, she stopped, turned around toward me, and started taking off things, sort of like when you take off clothes, but this time she told me she was taking off her Fears. "Oh, I don't need these. What was I thinking?" And she promptly, and joyfully dropped them one by one. They fell like rain, and then became raindrops, and then became beautiful teardrops - which, she said, are teardrops of Compassion. "They unite all of us in understanding, and caring. They create our beautiful Humanity."

Then, before my eyes, the tips of each teardrop became beautiful petals - Rose petals. There were many Rose petals. (Looking back now, I think about how much she liked the Double-Delight roses I'd brought her from my garden. After they bloomed, I was going to bring her the extra petals even if the rose wasn't fully intact.)

After seeing the raindrops turn into Rose petals, I opened my eyes for a moment, only to see Don standing on the other side of Dee, drumming with me! It was such a beautiful moment of warmth, and as I filled Don in with what Dee was showing me, we then closed our eyes and proceeded to drum some more together. What an incredible thing, to feel his love surround his sweet wife, Dee, and fill her heart to overflowing. Then Sunny stood with us, opening her heart and letting her love flow into Dee, too. I felt Dee's spirit strengthen magnificently then, and realized this unconditional love was releasing Dee and helping her powerfully expand into the Love that was blooming around her and inside her. Don and Sunny gave something so extraordinary that I felt forever changed by their heroic acts, by the unselfish love they shared through their tears.

Before I stopped drumming, I glanced up ahead of Dee, to see what she was looking at. I had felt the energy of many Angels in the golden light. They were everywhere. Everywhere. But on the Other Side of the Bridge was another treat for the beauty-loving Dee. Before her stood not worries nor fears, but a glorious Rose Garden. Many Rose bushes, each a different color. Blooming so brightly. Welcoming her Home.

Not surprisingly, Dee asked if we could have Rose petals at her Celebration of Life.

In the days before this, I had wondered how Dee's spirit would contact us from the Other Side. We'd talked about it, and she hadn't decided. I think she liked the mystery. "Well, Dee," I said, taunting her pragmatically, "You don't have to choose just *one* sign, only one way to let us know you're around us. You can choose more than one!" We'd laughed at this expansive, creative thought. Now, as I keep seeing this Bridge in my mind, I realize her signs of being with us have already begun. In my heart, I can only call this Bridge a Rainbow Bridge. This Bridge had a whole spectrum of Love in it - a veritable RAINBOW of Light that can heal us and lead us during the many different Passages of our lives!

Then tonight, as I was writing this story, my friend John suddenly told me he had a lucky thing to give me. He rarely interrupts me when he sees my fingers flying over the computer keys. Walking quickly toward me, he held a piece of paper over a small bowl. "What?" I stammered, a little disconcerted. Bending to give it to me, he grinned, and took the paper off. To my utter surprise, in the middle of my living room on a rainy October night with no open window in sight, came a bright red *Ladybug!* It bounced from the small glass bowl onto my fingers, made me giggle, and then flew upward - and twirled in delight. Who knows where it landed! *I only know I'll see it again . . .*

I took rose petals to Dee's beautiful Celebration of Life. And since then, I have seen her spirit twice. She's been off to my side, sitting one time on a stool at a restaurant counter. It's like this: you see a person. You immediately think, "There's Dee!" And then you remember Dee is on the Other Side - but in a heartbeat, you know it WAS Dee! That's the way it works. They get you, then they're gone, just like Allen as he waved at me from the side of the road beside his Schwan's truck. A glimmer, a wisp, a dream, a puzzle piece - and then they're back across the gossamer Veil. But they have your attention!

In such thoughtful ways, our Loved Ones continue to create Bridges - bridges that step us up into refreshingly new, higher dimensions of Love.

But they're so inventive, so creative - I have to grin. They are part of my heart, part of the Centerpoint of my Peace. With their love from above, they are helping me understand this "Mystery School of Grief". With their strong new Wings, they are helping me with my Mastery . . .

Chapter Sixteen

Mastery

Secret Number 31:
Mastery is not perfection.
Mastery is the ongoing act
of offering up our imperfection,
so we might continually BE perfected.

Secret Number 32:
The secret of Mastery
is to have a beginner's mind.

Secret Number 33:
Mastery is the Heartfelt Desire,
after being Healed,
to become the Healer,
to Give after you have been Given To.

Secret Number 34:
Mastery is
to Surrender to the More.

We come into this "Mystery School of Grief" as students. And hopefully, we will continue to be students. With an open heart, we ask Spirit what to do next in the many life tests we face. With a brave Avatar's sense of adventure, we ask what we are to learn. As we slow down and breathe in, we start receiving, and noticing. And with new eyes, we see the steps on our path. We see a Quest that involves our whole being, both our pains, and the insights and love that can come forth during our efforts. From a new vantage point we see both sides, the Yin and the Yang of life, and we decide to be part of the Healing Circle of Love, the Medicine Circle that reconnects us in beautifully mysterious ways.

Mastery is not the act of striving to be perfect. Instead, as stated in Chapter 12, it is called "The Sacred Practice." It is the practice of aligning ourselves with Wisdom and Light, which creates a further healing energy within us. As we caringly practice what we learn by applying these insights in our daily living, the healthy, healing forces of Love are strengthened within us. This process strengthens our spirit, and then ripples out to positively affect others like a stone causes a ripple in a pond. Healers know "The Practice" is the pathway to healing - and is the center of it. So healing can come in a million different ways as it radiates within you - and then radiates outward to others in any way Spirit directs. At times, it may be expressed in a word or in a deed, and at other times it may be activated as healing energy in our prayers or deep healing meditations.

Just as night follows day, it is natural that after we learn, we want to serve. It will happen at our own Pace, at our own Time. Don't worry, Mastery and the sense of Peace and Wisdom it provides is something that will come and go - but the difference is, you'll know it. That's Mastery - when you know you're off kilter, and you decide to center yourself, and begin again, with Love. And that's Heroic.

So Mastery is one part continuing to heal ourselves, and one part, passing on healing to others.

Along our path of healing from grief, we've changed. We've expanded. So now we want to cherish our Loved One's presence in our daily lives, by letting the Sunshine of what they stand for into our Intentions and Actions. This is a Pivotal Point - a point where a new kind of healing and expansion shows itself. For as we learn how to care for our own spirit and open up to whole new dimensions of Love, we realize we can share this Healing Energy with others.

Spirit will guide us as to whom we are destined to share this Sunshine with, but as we can immediately see - just being part of the new kind of Sunshine from our Loved Ones and Spirit, casts a bright light everywhere. Some people will see it in your smile. They will see how you've faced pain, yet have found something that brightens you, from the inside, out. They will see it in your gentleness, in your kind gestures, and in the way you may reach out and call them before they call you when they are in need. Spirit will place these needs in your heart. They are needs your heart will be called to fill. They will be your beautiful assignments only you are meant to fulfill. And they will be given to you, because of your walk with your Loved Ones, and because of the honor you have attained. It is a great thing.

As we can see, there are many reasons to love whom we love, and to share that love in the biggest of ways. Instead of Letting Our Loved Ones Go, we Let Our Loved Ones In, in this beautiful way of Spirit, which is life-giving. Jackie Chan's character of the drunken scholar in the movie, "The Forbidden Kingdom," said it something like this: *"One does not attach himself to people and desires, but then does he ever truly live?"*

Our Loved Ones are in our hearts for a reason. They've already made a big impact - AND they want to make more - by continuing to give us an abundance of Love. Love that naturally overflows, and wants to be shared. This is the kind of Love that honors our pain, and turns it into compassion. It is called the pain of the Wounded Warrior.

Secret Number 35:
The pain of the Wounded Warrior
becomes the Healing Light of Compassion
that calls a Multitude of Angels into Action.
Directing our Suffering into Healing
is how we get our Wings.

In life, all of us suffer, but it is what we do with it that counts. How we direct our energies. Our actions can be life-numbing, or life-enhancing. As we take a Sacred Pivot, we see Life before us. We see our Purpose(s). And we see all the particular people and all the events that are OURS - our opportunities to step up our own game and be part of any kind of healing that wants to occur. Once again, Spirit is wanting our involvement, so we can co-create with this Higher Level of Love.

When we lift up our eyes from grief, a whole world appears before us. As Henry David Thoreau so wisely said, *"Only a day dawns to which we are awake."* During this Mastery stage, we are given many ways to earn our "angel wings" while here on Earth. But just as I wondered if I could help the Healer turn the energy flow direction around for my friend, you also will wonder if you can do it. Are you good enough? Do you have the skills, or the experience?

Fortunately, perfection is not the key. Remember, even the Dalai Lama wears glasses! And all of us will find we need Higher Guidance. It's the human condition. Also, Higher Guidance is especially important when we are healing from grief. It is the key that wisely helps us convert darkness into new understandings, and new Light. In this way, it is an alchemical process. A conversion on the grandest of scales. It is the gold that will warm our heart, and bring it back to life. That's why it is a holy journey. As Jim so wisely puts it:

> *"Sometimes when you let go of the darkest parts of yourself,*
> *you allow your lightest parts to become lighter."*

If we are Wounded Warriors, we are being called into action, into loving action. This is *a Master Class for the Soul,* and our decisions affect ourselves and others in profound ways. *There is a way to grieve with fear, and there is a way to grieve with Love. When we choose Love, the whole Universe lines up behind us.* A multitude of Angels await the invitation to be of greater service in our lives. They cheer when we want to be a Catalyst for something Good!

As I write this, the area around my dining room table gets warm. I take off my morning sweater (ah, my "mourning" sweater), and turn off the gas fireplace. I open the sliding glass door to the outside, and invite my cat, Bella, to enjoy the fresh air. To me, it reflects the same way we get warmed by Spirit's Love, until we feel good inside, and open the door to the fresh air that wants to fill our lungs.

As we continue our path of healing, and then sharing that healing, we learn to take a sacred in-breath (in so many ways), and receive from a place so centered, it is our life core, and as we feel that peace, we learn how to ever get back to that place of peace. As the mystic poet from India, Kabir, once said, *"What is God? He is the breath inside the breath."*

And when we center ourselves, and begin the Divine in-breath, we open up our Spiritual Curiosity. *We ask, "What does Spirit have to say? What does Spirit want to teach me in this series of events?"* These questions naturally lead us deeper, for in all the different kinds of in-breaths in which we receive from the Divine, we learn something that is just beyond the scope of our knowledge. We get Surprises, Surprises from Spirit that take us further into the Heart of Spirit, and the Heart of Healing. In my dream journal, I see a series of Dreams which increased my understanding, and surprised me.

"The Koan"

My notes in my dream journal begin, interestingly, with a drawing - two drawings actually. They are simple drawings. Imagine two rectangular boxes, one resting perfectly on top of the other. The box next to it, drawn second, is a bigger box, which is now square. The important insight here is that the second, bigger box, is made from the two smaller boxes - combined. In the dream, it goes on to give its own definition of a Koan:

A Koan (and it shows the two smaller boxes): a problem, held in the palm of your hand for a day, then reveals its enlightenment.

At the end of the dream it says something important that I mentioned earlier. It means a lot to me. It adds:

For example,

alone = all-one, (as I had found in the dream dictionary).

This is an insightful dream to me, because I wasn't clear about what a Koan was before this. When the word showed up in my dream, I was surprised, and wanted to find out more about it. New words happen in dreams sometimes.

I think a Koan is a problem we're given. As in the concept of Yin and Yang, the challenges and the dualities of what we feel, and what we are to learn (thus, two boxes), are sacred. When we follow the path of trying to understand them, we need to open our heart and see something bigger (thus, the big box formed by the two smaller boxes). That's when they come together to form something new, which will be a Blessing. It is a Blessing first given to us, and a Blessing meant to touch others. That is what is meant by being a Healer. It takes many forms of expression.

My gentle, light-filled acupuncturist, Aram Levendosky, and I talk about such things. He said, "Yes, this is about the interplay of the Problem and the Solution, and also, the Koan itself, because of its very Mystery, is meant to wake us up! It's used during meditation for just that purpose."

"Ahhh, yes!" I said. "The Koan is meant to wake us up! As it does, it can take us on a journey of discovery. And that's why this journey is "The *Mystery* School of Grief!" It is meant to wake us up, smack dab into the middle of our lives, where all great mysteries reside - waiting to expand our ways of thinking, into something bigger.

And one of the most beautiful Koans to crack is that ALONE means ALL-ONE.

The next dream about Mastery rode the waves of the Koan Dream, the same night. The words are exactly as it was written in my dream journal.

"The Alchemy of Love"

I had been walking with a turbulence for a time. The different boxes (in the Koan dream) were meant to be combined. This is to Create. (Again, it shows 2 rectangular boxes, one on top of the other, with a slight space in between - like breathing room - this time.)

I realize I have now discovered/have been taught the alchemical process of how to create, how to make Love happen.

The separate boxes were combinations, containing problems and solutions. When I asked Spirit for help, many Angels were activated and happy to be involved.

I have a son. I am teaching him/have taught him how to create Love.

I point at a Lavender Blooming Tree to begin my instruction.

This demonstrates how our problems are designed with a matching interlocking puzzle piece of understanding. Our problems, when dealt with in a sacred manner, lead us to our new understandings (wise solutions). *Together, they fit like puzzle pieces or keys, and as we work on them - with the breath of Spirit - it allows Love to bloom inside what I will call the Lavender Blooming Tree of Us.*

In all things, we are guided. As we give Spirit breathing room to help us (by breathing in Spirit's Love), a new wisdom enters into our consciousness. As we step into The Practice of Mastery, we need not worry, the next steps will appear. If we wonder how we will learn new aspects of Healing, the answers and opportunities will unfold. In a way, the path becomes effortless, as we listen to the requests of our heart. For me, I felt a new desire - to more actively direct the great Energy of Love in a Healing Way. The next guidance was gifted to me during a deep meditation.

I see in my journal notes that beforehand, I had been on my way to a healing group in McMinnville, and I saw not one, not two, but three Red-Tailed Hawks - and then I saw two on my way back. I saw them up-close (again!). They swooped in and flew across my car, and then landed on a tall telephone pole near the highway, where I could be sure to see them. So, once home, I decided to meditate and let Allen through. It is a meditation I will never forget, as it opened up so many things in me, including so many ways to help healing occur. This is one of them.

Meditation:
"The Healing Golden Spiral"

As you know, I'd had a challenging relationship with my parents. It took them 2-3 years after they had passed over before they reconnected with me from the Other Side, and it tremendously helped heal my heart, and theirs. After this, I was inspired to do more. It is a simple meditation - maybe that's why it is a good meditation for all of us - but it is imbued with such a full force of healing golden Light, that it is good to imagine the full import of it as you read about it. Let yourself feel the warm, loving, ever expanding Light in it.

In the meditation, Allen and I reached up and brought down the Healing Golden Spiral of Love from above. This is a life-changing kind of Light, and the Golden Spiral radiates with the warmth of Unconditional Love. It was brought through the hearts of Allen and myself, in combination. I have a drawing in my journal that shows how it came down in a Spiral. As the Healing Golden Spiral glowed in our heart area, it then expanded, and our hearts felt that incredibly loving and healing expansion. Like a radiator, The Golden Light reverberated with Love - and just as in the vision I was shown of Allen's "birth-day" on the Other Side, the warm, Golden Spiral sparkled with energy and healing.

As this Spiral of Healing, Golden Light came into my heart, and healed and expanded it, I was then directed to move it into my mom's heart. Then I held it there, with a loving hand, and let it do its work - so it could heal my mom. We were directed to let it take its time, and heal deeply. Let it become warm; let it gracefully expand. Then we were directed to slowly move the Healing Spiral of ever expanding Light back and forth, both to the right and to the left, to heal all that person's past and future. To heal all that came from the past generations, and to heal and make good all that would be passed to the future generations - as it wanted to heal everything! It was a healing of great magnitude. And once again, Spirit led Allen to help me. I think this was our first moment of actually working together, and it meant all the more because of it.

This meditation was significant, too, because it went back and forth in time. The expanding Spiral was very important, and I was told it was somewhat like a DNA Spiral. (In Sacred Geometry, the ever expanding spiral, exemplified by the Nautilus shell, is considered to reflect one of the foundational forms of Creation, and the spiritual design of the Universe. It also metaphysically alludes to the growth of one's spirit and its harmonic progression over time. The Nautilus is an example of how the progression of expansion of the spiraling shell perfectly creates harmonic ratios of psi. I'm not a mathematician nor an expert on Sacred Geometry, but this fascinates me.) During the meditation, the Healing Golden Spiral was healing deep into the many layers and levels of who we are (DNA), healing the core of our spirit.

This dream and the Healing Spiral itself were so powerful, I knew I could use the Golden Spiral on many occasions, for many different reasons. It is so powerful, it found a way to repeat itself, and bring me Confirmation. I was stunned when I went to the movies, and saw the Golden Spiral in the healing scenes in "Avatar." And shown with it was a healing Violet Flame, like the Lavender (Violet) Blooming Tree in my dream!   Since then, I have also attended a healing workshop based on bringing in "The Healing Violet Flame." And my friend, John, also experienced it in a dream, only his Spiral was Purple (like Violet), showing that the color can be unique, but the Spiral is there for all of us individually.   Such "coincidences!"

         After this, the Spiral continued in my dreams. (I tell you this to let you know these kinds of things can also happen to you. Each of us will receive our own types of healing insights and messages.) It showed up in another healing dream, in which the expanding Spiral of Golden Healing Light was paired with music - the enchanting, Gregorian Monk, Angel-like chanting that centers our spirit and causes it to soar. The Golden Light was brought in with the kind of harmonic, uplifting singing that opens our hearts. The combination of the Spiral and the ethereal chanting/singing then entered a sacred Pyramid shape (I hadn't studied pyramids, either).

         In this rarified place, the music was amplified beyond measure. The healing, contained now in this powerful vessel, took on great healing power. It reverberated, and was magnified with Love beyond measure. And in this beautiful place, deep in the pyramid where it should be dark, it was Light. It was shining and beaming with a Light that changed things.

         I have since learned the Spiral was used in the design of the pyramids!

         If you want to know how to use the Healing Golden Spiral of Light after this kind of meditation, then use what you've come to know as my "Reiki Hands." Take the time to fully center yourself, and fully feel the meditation, then let that Divine Light of Lights flow through your heart, down into your hands - and then through your hands to the person you care for. Let the Golden Healing Spiral help you, and let the reverberations in something like the symbolic Pyramid add to the magnitude. Then let yourself be guided as to what you feel and what you hear - and what loving insights may come through. You may receive insights right then, or much later. But just feeling the Love and the good energy of healing is enough -

more than enough, for both yourself and for the person you're sending good energy to!

My purpose in sharing this Golden meditation with you, is that you may also practice it, in your own way, and find your own illuminations. My friend, John Judy, did just that immediately after he read about the meditation. He added, "Basically, It prompted my own meditation and in it a Koan was posed. It asked 'What is the difference between a Circle and a Spiral?' The insights that came to me noted how each one has the Yin and the Yang; each has two sides - and they return. The Circle returns to the same place, closes and completes itself; the Spiral returns to another place (either above or below its point of origin), so the Spiral is moving forward whereas the Circle stays in place. And so the Spiral becomes a way to go between two worlds. As we state our prayer or meditation, energy passes upward from us in a Spiral, and Energy comes downward in the Spiral from Great Spirit and our Loved Ones on the Other Side. A Circle stays in place; it stays on one side of the Veil, as in a friendship or a relationship that forms a Circle. A Circle is between you and I or two objects on one side of the Veil, and a Spiral contains healing Energy that goes both ways, back and forth between the Veil. In this way, the potent energy contained within the Circle is released into a great Spiral of Healing. In that way, it is a Circle that completes itself! And in this endless, transforming Circle, we Forever grow."

As you might recall from my Dream Journal, a Koan is a problem, held in the palm of your hand for a time, which then reveals its enlightenment.

After sharing these insights with me, John opened the book, "Messages from Forever; a Novel of Aboriginal Wisdom" by Marlo Morgan, and read, "Human life is a spiral, we come from forever (the Other Side of the Veil) and we return there, we hope at a higher level. Time is a circle and our relationships are also circles." (The thoughts in parentheses are from John.)

The aborigines say our life is Forever; and that we are constantly growing and we come to this side of the Veil to learn in real time. And so we Spiral in and out of both sides of the Veil in order for our spirit to expand.

Suffice it to say that some aboriginal healers came in recently to help John successfully combat a lung disease! Spirit sends its power in mysterious ways! I love imagining our prayers, for example, as potent Circles, which seek expression. And the Spiral as that great exchange: our potent energy meeting Spirit's grand healing Energy. As the Spiral moves upward, and is met by Spirit, then a whole host of vibrant healing Energy Spirals back downward into our awaiting arms.

Just think what will happen as more of us practice this beautiful, impactful Golden Spiral Meditation, and even more healing Energy is activated!

Healing is exciting, for that reason - because it is a pivotal place. It is the power-point of Change. Another way to let Healing Change occur is to listen to the sound of something like a Native American drum, as music helps conduct healing energies. Just a few months ago, in my "Writing - for the Life of It" column, I wrote about the process:

"As I played my Native American drum recently, I unexpectedly learned more about Change. First, the drum tells us to 'listen to it.' Yes, when you're playing a Native drum, you realize Change can be listened to. It has a beat, a rhythm - and each set of Changes that comes up for you in your life holds gifts for you, and each one has its own unique rhythm. And that made me listen.

Secondly, as I listened and played, I discovered a drumbeat that actually initiates Change. I was beating the drum with two drumsticks, and when I wanted to make one unified drumbeat, I noticed one drumstick sometimes hit slightly before the other. *Ta-da (flam in drumming terms)*. And this slightly overlapping set of beats, I understood, was the sound that creates or strengthens Change! It is a symbolic energetic movement that is very powerful and helpful. It's like telling the Universe you want the Change. You 'get it' and are moving into it.

After you play this *ta-da*, you can then play around with having both drumsticks hit in unison, which is symbolic of actually harmonizing with your dream. You see your dream in its beautiful expression. But there is no getting there without the dynamic stepping stones of fresh, drumbeat-like actions that upset the status quo and make way for the new thoughts and visions to come in."

That's why, in Reiki, I am directed to listen to the different places in a person's body. They hold the angst, or the block, or the problem. Identifying the pain is part of letting it go, and releasing it into higher hands than our own.

So how do we get there - to this harmonious place where healing can happen?

> *"Center yourself in Love,*
> *and you will find Peace."*

When we truly center ourselves in Love, we enter a place of Innocence. If we come as a child, we can enter a kingdom of Peace that knows no bounds. (Based on Matthew 19:14). And as the Beginner's Mind proposes, we need to enter with an Attitude of *Openness, Eagerness,* and with a *Lack of Preconceptions.*

If we simply center ourselves by breathing-in Love, we open our bodies to the fresh air of healing. If we move this warm, golden Light of Love through the different places in our body, we start to be guided by Love. We naturally start to Match Love. And as we take time to feel this Golden Light within our heart, we open to the richness of new insights and ideas from Spirit. This Openness brings many Ah-Ha's our way. These are personal, exquisitely pertinent Ah-Ha's, too.

No wonder, as we practice prayer and meditation, we develop an attitude of Eagerness. This attitude also helps us set down our Monkey Mind, our mind that is constantly worrying, and finding the worst in things. This negative mindset is actually one caused from Perfectionism. And as we are learning, the point is not to be Perfect, but to let ourselves become Perfected. Remember, even the wisest person will experience grief, so we will all need help at some point. Reaching out for help *is* Wisdom.

The only way to begin the process of Perfecting our soul, is to use our worries and Negatives in a new way. When we are centered, we can constructively pour out our most painful, authentic emotions. When we pour these authentic emotions out *into the hands of Spirit,* then it becomes a Sacred Devotion, a sacred offering. In this way, we surrender our limiting ego, and opt for something more. And all the insights we receive because we have set our limiting fears and preconceptions aside, will bring untold, helpful Surprises to us!

After I painted a Fall Leaf in all its colorful glory, I was inspired to entitle it: *"The Beauty of Falling."* Then I made a greeting card out of it, and on the back, I added:

Falling in love . . .
Falling for a good idea . . .
Falling by letting go & letting in,
gracefully surrendering to something Higher,
and in that instant, becoming
B o u y a n t   a n d   L i g h t.

Mastery is ongoing. It is not a one-night stand, but is more akin to looking at the Milky Way. The more you look, the more stars you see.

Eventually, you begin to see you are connected. In an amazing way, everything is helping you.

And indeed, you are a part of the Milky Way.

So, of course, we know we are not alone. And our Loved Ones know that too. They find all kinds of ways to reflect that back to us, star by shining star.

Chapter Seventeen

Life's Surprises:
The Red-Tailed Hawk & John

Secret Number 36:
Never Say Your Life is Over;
It is Ever a Beautiful, Purposeful Work in Progress,
so Stay Open to Surprises.

After we have experienced great loss, life's Purpose often feels as if it's been shaken out of us. "What do we do now?" we ask ourselves, even when we still have family or friends here who need our love and attention. As we know so well now, our Loved Ones on the Other Side are one-of-a-kind. Because we realize no one is ever replaceable, we may understandably miss them and be tempted to "stop action," and in essence, stop our lives. But as our Loved Ones from the Other Side tend us, they are often the ones who point us toward our ongoing Purposes. No one will ever replace our Loved Ones, but our Loved Ones want the love we had experienced with them before their passing to continue living within the heartbeats of our lives. If we let them, they will help us hear the purposes that will come from connecting with people and projects that call our name. Our job is to listen. In doing so, we honor the spirits of our Loved Ones, and forge entire new projects with them.

Secret Number 37:
Do Not Judge your Ongoing Purposes;
Embrace each Relationship & Project,
and Let your Loved One Help You with it.

Our next Purpose(s) may be different relationships, or projects that benefit those around us. In my case, I didn't know if I would have another love relationship or not. So I looked at the whole spectrum of opportunities with people, pets, and projects Spirit put before me. I paid special attention to my family and friends, and then felt drawn to teach writing to a great group of seniors. Even as I sought to serve them, their friendships softened my days and inspired me as they read their life stories and made my laughter return. With each step, I continued listening to my intuition, and so it was that my life continued with meaning.

Then, after many years of being on my own, I was surprised to feel Spirit place the desire for a new love relationship in my heart. Allen had died at just 57, and now, years later, here I was in my sixties. What a time to start over! I had to laugh, but at the same time, when you're in your sixties you understand how young you are. Maybe people in their twenties don't understand it, but as you grow older, you understand what a rich time it is, and how you have even more to offer.

It was just after Spirit placed this new path in my heart that I went to a meeting where intuitive Candia Sanders was speaking. After her talk, she asked, "Are there any questions?"

When I raised my hand, I was quite surprised. Before I had time to ask my question, Candia was looking straight at me. She smiled, her eyes warm and sparkling, as she confidently said, "Yes, you will have another relationship!"

Big grin from Candia.

I had never met Candia before and she knew nothing about me, not even my name. It was quite the night! We talked a bit afterward, and I soon had a session with her. Over the years she has been a valuable mentor to me, and we also become fast friends.

With this new knowledge, I had to get beyond my own shyness, and open myself up to a whole new journey. I had to practice this new art of dating. But along the way, I experienced dreams of guidance, and serendipitous events galore. I told myself, "At the very least I will make new friends." And I did.

But I also began to understand how life has surprises for us, if only we point ourselves forward. As I dated, I even did some online dating (for the most part - ergh!). Then, after quite some time, a shift suddenly occurred, and Candia called to say "There's someone I want you to meet," which created a whole series of surprises, including even more surprising kinds of guidance - from Red-Tailed Hawks! Candia told me how she had been sitting beside this long-time friend of hers, John, and she saw a vision of us walking and flirting with each other beside the Metolius River, just next to where he lived!

Before long, John and I graduated from email and were having long, interesting phone calls with each other. Eventually I read this to my seniors writing group:

"The Red-Tailed Hawk, More than a Friend"

Soon after the first fun words flew between us, John and I talked about the Red-Tailed Hawks. As a river guide, he saw them often, so like me, he knew them. They had been coming to me and guiding me for many years by then, through the trials of widowhood. Then, just days before John first visited me from Central Oregon, a hawk melodiously sang to me at the break of dawn - telling me something.

S c r e e . . . s c r e e . . . the hawk sang evocatively, like the first notes of a new day; like a sonnet - a proclamation of Something Important coming my way.

During John's visit to my area, as we drove next to the stretch of meadows nearby, he pointed out a Red-Tailed Hawk flying near us - one I had missed.

"See," John said with a twinkle in his eye, "You're not the only one who sees the Red-Tailed Hawks." At that time, I had not told John how I had first seen the Bald Eagle, and then the Red-Tailed Hawks right at this very place after Allen's passing.

But even after this, maybe because we were not quite ready yet, we decided to become just friends - good friends who helped each other out - and cared. So it was that I ignored the Red-Tailed Hawks and kept going a different direction. I dated others and sometimes told John of my exploits. One time a sudden emergency caused me to cancel a date with a fellow I was just getting to know who lived out-of-town. My son's wonderful cat had become grievously ill, and even though we dashed her to the nearest veterinary hospital open on a Sunday, she died in his arms that sober afternoon. What a shock! During this devastating event, I was so glad I was there for my son, Jim. But my potential date did not seem to think this was "ample reason" to postpone our date. He was a huge jerk, exceedingly argumentative and demeaning, so I knew I never wanted to see him again. I wanted to shrug it off, but as a parent, I was pretty steamed, and I was still processing his lack of care for my son.

But as I was able to vent about this on the phone with John, he had a brilliant solution. "If he's gonna be that immature," he said simply, "we'll just send him a box of diapers!"

Immediately, as I imagined this other guy opening a whole big box of diapers, all my frustration evaporated, and I was laughing my head off. John was proving to be a good friend. Someone who had my back and could ease the tensions of life.

As time went on, I was still dating. The current new fellow was nice but was proving to be boring, boring, boring. What can you do? Who wants to be bored for the rest of their lives?! It was then I began hearing John's name above the others, so I picked up my things, made my excuses, and promptly left the date I was on with the boring fellow! As my foot hit the pedal, I wondered what all this meant, and zoomed onto the freeway back to Portland, exceedingly glad to be a free woman with choices - only to hear the serendipitous "Beep" of the nicest text from John!

"I'm driving through some open fields and I'm surrounded by *dozens* of Red-Tailed Hawks."

This captured my attention, and finally, not long thereafter, I accepted John's kind offer to visit him. During my stay, John confidently drove me up some tricky gravel roads to the very top of a ski resort-mountain he worked at, and just before we reached the summit, some strong wings flew in front of our windshield. (Here we go, with windshields again!) Still, I had a hard time believing it when I realized it was a magnificent Red-Tailed Hawk - and then the majestic creature flew right beside us, and even landed just feet away on a tall white ski run marker on John's side. I watched, smiling, as John rolled down his window, boldly stopped his Ford Explorer, and warmly said, "Hi Fella!"

The stately hawk sat there for a minute, seemingly very comfortable with us, as if it could take time to share tea. Then the powerful Red-Tailed Hawk stretched out its broad wings and flew beside my window - again! - just feet away. I felt as if my fingers could have touched it. "How can this be?" I thought. It felt as if myself and the Red-Tailed Hawk flew together, in tandem, for one long moment in time . . .

As my eyes finally left the soaring wings of our Red-Tailed Hawk, I looked over to where it had previously perched, and read the ski run marker . . . "Leap of Faith," it said!

I chuckled, finally acknowledging all of these "coincidences." And I took a leap of faith that started me on a journey into love with John.

John and I both opened our hearts, and with some starts and stops, rolled into our future. Allen's guidance was felt many times as Red-Tailed Hawks directed my path, and as you can see, *it definitely began to feel as if the Red-Tailed Hawks were also from John.*

Both John and I had much healing going on. New relationships, no matter at what age, can be awkward and challenging on many levels. But just as John and I found our way to each other, we found our way into the deeper learnings available to each of us through the sacred portal of relationships. As seniors, we look at this new landscape and know we're not done learning. That's why it is very valuable to stay in the mix of life, connected to purposeful relationships of all kinds. It does good things for your heart.

I write this to show how, after we lose someone we love, Spirit is not through with us. It is wise not to judge what form our relationships, projects and purposes take, for each one is sacred and beautiful, and each one opens up different ways for us to learn and grow. For some of us, we may open ourselves up to a love relationship, and for others (including John or myself later on, depending on which one of us passes over first), we will also have great, great purpose with our family and friends, and projects that bring sunshine to others. And, of course, many of these people-purposes can happen at the same time. As I look back upon Secret Number 34, I see what Spirit is saying to all of us, each in our own way: *Mastery is to Surrender to the More.* Just as Spirit surprises us during meditation time, Spirit will continue to surprise us with some blessings of the heart. And if we are truly wise, we will feel our Loved Ones on the Other Side guiding us along the way, generously filling our footsteps with ever-expanding constellations of their Love. And in this way, in our own hearts and in the hearts of those we touch, Love will be multiplied. And our Loved Ones will be proud.

Chapter Eighteen

Double Rainbows

I began wanting to call this last chapter, Double Rainbow. Singular. But Spirit opened the windows further. Double Rainbows (plural) are reflective of so many good things, times two, or times ten thousand. The repetitive nature of these mini-miracles within our lives breaks through our natural doubts and tells us we do not stand alone: we have help. We have help in a myriad of ways, some of which we see softly as a physical Double Rainbow appears out of the clouds, and reminds us our Loved One is near. And in other ways, our mini-miracles appear right in front of us, as friends help us by reflecting so many things Spirit is conveying to us. We get "emergency packages" sent to us all the time, if only we notice them. We get Double Rainbows, Double Blessings, and Double Confirmations.

Secret Number 38:
*If you Notice Mini-Miracles
and Creative Messages from your Loved One,
then they happen More Often.*

It's much like how communication works here on the Earth Plain. If someone talks to you and you don't talk back, they eventually lose the incentive to talk with you. On the Other Side, they are always there, but they respect your free will and your decisions. So if you want to hear more from them, chat with them. Respect their efforts to reach you, and in your own way, answer them. Let them know you appreciate their efforts to show you love and continue sending them love. It's like visiting a gravesite. Let yourself have a chat; let yourself spend healthy time with them and commune a bit. As time goes by, if you notice the mini-miracles and messages they send, they will naturally expand. After years of listening to the ways Allen communicates with me, I am quite used to it. It's a beautiful part of my life.

Secret Number 39:
Be Grateful.
Concentrate on Celebrating
all the Good Things in your Loved One
and let that Good continue to Flow into Your Life.

One of the ways to let Double Rainbows in is to concentrate on the good - especially the good things about your Loved One. Being grateful allows all of the Higher Energies to align with yours. Being grateful is the big tip-off to the Divine Universe that says you are ready to receive. Being grateful changes the equation and changes the tenor of our days. So let yourself frequently celebrate all the good in your Loved One. List the things you love about him or her. Let your Loved One hear your grateful voice or thoughts. This works on all levels of our lives, and the harmony will bring about even greater good.

When I was sad about Allen, I would think about all the good things, about all the things I loved about him, and it stopped my downward spiral. Even the smallest list of good things can create a gentle, honest upward spiral of thought. It eased my mind many a day, and brought me closer to Allen. I could literally feel his happiness as I did so. And that is one way Allen has become such a part of the fabric of my life.

As was mentioned in the last chapter, blessings have a way of multiplying. I thought I was done conveying all these Double Confirmations, but Spirit wants them to come your way, like your own special emergency package. Please read them to relax and see the joyous nature of these double-bonuses and blessings, but also read this chapter when you're tired and your spirit needs uplifting.

As I said in the beginning, this walk of healing from grief is not an easy one, the tests are great, and sometimes we will need to replenish our spirit. But now it is revealing to look back on our journey in The Mystery School of Grief, and see how we have dynamically increased the circumference of our hearts. And how we have developed the most beautiful kind of strength. We have honored Love instead of Fear, and we have developed a gentle Courage that leads ourselves and others upward.

Secret Number 40:
When you develop gentle Courage,
You make an Upward Shift.
You become an Integral Part
of Countless
Double Rainbows.

Now, after reading and experiencing these Secrets, you are a PART of the beautiful Mysteries you have received. And these are the Healing Mysteries your heart will share.

I want to thank each person who has been traveling through The Mystery School of Grief. I want to thank you because it does take Courage. This poem is from me, for each of you, and for our Loved Ones on the Other Side, too. It was written before Allen passed over, when we stayed at a wonderful bed and breakfast beside the sparkling McKenzie River. May you read about the flight of this courageous Mallard Duck and celebrate the Double Blessings of your Loved Ones and of yourself, as you demonstrate a "lift-off" of your spirit, and the Courage each of us have now because we have chosen Love instead of Fear:

"Shaman's Flight"

"And what do you say
of Fear?" I asked.
And the river answered
"Look out upon my ripples . . ."

A bird then circled in
downstream and dove
into a flight path
all its own.

Inches off the river's

white-water it flew
as if on a mission,
unparalleled.

Still, a common bird
I thought it to be
until it rocketed
past me -
a flash of emerald
green,
a shaman's flight.

Its Mallard wings
whispering
showing me all things -
even courage of my own -
that I would miss
if I gave Fear
my heart, my soul.

Thank you, dear fellow travelers, for being courageous. It becomes you. It looks good on you - and we want to thank our Loved Ones for their courage in helping us choose Love instead of Fear, too. After all, we could have shunned their light touches of Love. We could have closed the door, and not thought about all the Love they still have to give from the Other Side.

The concept of being Double Blessed is reflected in another dream I had. It happened at the coast, at my friend, Sue's beautiful beach house. It was a soothing visit, a great getaway. One morning I woke up with this unforgettable dream of being tended:

"*The Mirror of Heaven and Earth*"

Allen, like a tall beam of energy, is thinking of me in Heaven. (Then there is a drawing of one tall oval of energy in Heaven, and a mirror oval of it on Earth, in Life.)

Then Allen is showing me how his loving energy is touching me here on Earth (there is a place in the drawing, where the two ovals meet and merge, like a horizon line). And how his loving energy is flowing through my friends, and those around me, too - to care for me.

The ongoing loving energy going from Heaven to Earth is one part of the Double Blessing, as the Love from Allen is mirrored here on Earth. Without this dream, could I have even imagined such beautiful tending?

I hope you are applying all these messages to yourself, too. That's why I'm sharing them. The dream itself was a gift I cherish, and this "mirroring" dream also demonstrates another beautiful pattern of how Spirit plans for these puzzle pieces to go together over time, because this dream wholeheartedly reminds me of the article I wrote - this time about a Great Blue Heron, standing in the pond, his image *mirroring both Heaven and Earth*, guiding me to know more about both sides of the Veil.

This goes further, as it falls together in the loveliest of ways. As I work on the book, in my journal I find a beautiful dream message from Allen, from the Other Side.

In my dream, I have a conversation with Allen:

I ask Allen, "Why is it me left here, to what purpose?"

"This is our Life's Work," I hear him gently say. "It is to be a Double Rainbow, so people will know the Other Side, and another Dimension of Love."

What can I say? What a beautiful thing for me to receive - and then discover later in my journal! As I worked on this book, it definitely became a Sacred Devotion that Allen and I wanted to bring to you (and now John is part of this Sacred Devotion, too), and it definitely has brought some personal dividends my way. (You really won't believe this - as I edit this chapter late on a Saturday night, I look up at the news. On the weather portion, they're showing a photo of a Double Rainbow! Even I can hardly believe this!)

I also received a Double Confirmation of our love and devotion when I opened a thoughtful, artistic card Jim had given me years ago. It has a branch of Cherry Blossoms on the front of it. Inside, Jim writes this about me and Allen:

> *Every petal a stone,*
> *building a bridge between*
> *Heaven and Earth;*
> *Dad's will be done,*
> *that you see his love*
> *this day.*

Wow, can Jim write! Both Julian and Jim gave me wonderful cards of support during this entire time, and I did the same for them. Every word counted. Sometimes the boys made me sigh in such a good way, and sometimes they made me laugh. It is all so healing for all three of us!

I think about how my journey started out so unclear, and is now *so real*. Each sacred event, and each word of help, and each Double Rainbow has created a journey into a new, more spacious kind of Love - and it is Real. Somewhere along the line, pretty early on, this was highlighted when I went to a spiritual book study group with Jim. It included some wise people who sensed the deeper levels of existence. As I spoke with one bright, kind woman about "losing" Allen, she looked at me. Her eyes were bright as she spoke to me of the passing over of one of her good friends. We spoke about the new things I was experiencing, as Allen reached out to soften my grief.

"Yes!," she answered enthusiastically. And then she said some words that have stuck with me all these years. She looked into my eyes and said,

> "It's as if they are *more real now.*
> *In an amazing way, they are more real than before!*"

At that time, this was a lot to absorb, but it motivated me to continue letting Allen in, and to listen to all he was giving to me. As I looked out at the Rose Garden in my backyard one night, I paused to say goodnight to my Roses. I glanced at both the light pink and the ivory moon-like petals, seen so clearly as they glowed even in the nightfall, and in one instant, I knew how *real* Allen was now, that whether seen or unseen, his presence was with me, even on the Other Side. Here's a portion of the poem I wrote:

> "*. . . Whether seen or unseen,*
> *whether in dusk, or sun, or darkest night,*
> *whether awake or in deepest sleep,*
> *the Roses never stop their blooming.*
>
> *So it is that tonight, I close my eyes,*
> *quietly tracing the fragrance of Rose petals*
> *on my pillow,*
> *knowing that Blooming is for Me.*"

When I merely open my heart, I become part of a bigger world. And in another dream from my journal, I experience how the distance between one world and the other continues to beautifully evaporate:

"Two Chairs"

I had gone to my good friend and intuitive, Bev, but on my own I now see and feel into this new realm.

Allen came and touched me, many times, to let me know he was beside me, just a shift of energy away. It was like just he and I were there. In a chair, we are side by side, shoulder to shoulder, and we look at each other and see each other.

"Like I am here," he said, "you are here. We are here together."

And in the spirit of Double Confirmations, no wonder I read this, by Kabir:

> "*Are you looking for me?*
> *I am in the next seat.*
> *My shoulder is against yours.*"

So many kinds of "Double Rainbows" throughout this celebratory chapter. I hope you can count them all! Spirit is doubling up on Dreams, and also the gifts within the dreams, that are linked together so evocatively:

"Young Again"

This year, I had another dream *in which I very clearly and very vividly saw Allen as a young man, about 20 years old. This was before I met him. It surprised me, as I'd never seen him this young before! In the dream, it seemed important that he showed himself this way.*

I had heard from others that our Loved Ones can take on a younger look on the Other Side, so this dream experience was interesting. I personally think they take on specific looks at different times to get our attention, or to give us a certain message. The younger look seems to give the message that they are ok, feeling good. I also thought back to how I actually saw Allen in the burgundy recliner in our family room. I saw him as Puzzle Pieces. And a few days ago my friend, Sally, in another form of Double Blessings, gave me a book with this quote by Corrie ten Boom:

"God knows and is interested both in the hardest problems we face and the tiniest details that concern us. He knows how to put everything in place, like a jigsaw puzzle, to make a beautiful picture."

Whether Allen showed himself as 20 years old, or as Puzzle Pieces, I feel that in all these ways, I am being cared for, as Allen's "Mirror" dream told me. As if to highlight all this help, I then received another dream, another touch of Love during the difficult nights of the soul. It came to me in the form of a poem, a dream/poem.

"I Hold This Candle for You"

At first - loss so hard.
Now - I see Allen holding
a candle, leading us all

forward into greater Light.

What a beautiful dream to receive! Allen is holding a candle for us . . .

In addition, I can't believe I'm even receiving short poems, too! Each dream helped me, each in its own way, and they added up like Sunshine that warmed my heart and soul. As I continued to heal, I made progress I could feel.

In the next dream, I gained the perspective (the Belvedere) of what the very purpose of being Double Rainbows means. (I also try to write out all these dreams just as I've so imperfectly scrawled them in my dream journal, usually in the middle of the night, or in the faint dawn of morning.) I love this dream.

"Along the Road"

(a group of us) We were all studying happiness. Our mates or Loved Ones (Allen) left (went to the Other Side) and we stayed along the road - and danced and taught people, by demonstration, the happiness of Love and Faith.

I think of all these wonderful synchronistic events as I return from lunch and glance down to see the bright penny I spoke about in the beginning of this book. I kept it in my car, to see me through the writing process. It almost winks at me in pleasure! Then I think of another healing intuitive, who suddenly started talking about pennies, "Pennies from Heaven," at a talk Jim and I went to. She said they're important. They have a job. "Since they are Cents (sense - as in good sense), they help you stay CENTered." She likes to make you giggle!

By the way, she added, as I talked with her alone afterward, "He (Allen) is right beside you - winking at you!" Sometimes these Double Confirmations really make you smile.

And then I also find my own notes in my journal. *"The other side of pain is peace (like a coin)."*

So many Pennies from Heaven!

Remember, Spirit is providing all these Double Confirmations for a reason. Our resistance can be great, even about receiving extraordinarily beautiful gifts placed right into our hands. I went on a walk to Cook's Park today, and paused to look at the Tualatin River from the vantage point of the bridge. I call this little, real life story:

"Two Turtles"

Today was one of the first sunny days of Spring. As I looked out on the far river bank of the Tualatin River, I saw some buddies: two turtles who were finally coming out from Winter's slumber, and soaking up the sunshine on their favorite log. I hadn't seen them since last Fall. They were each about 8" in diameter, so they made a statement, even from across the river.

Just as I was enjoying them, a family came along the bridge, and the whole family was excited when I told them about the two turtles. They told me how they had seen them last year, too. The young son with the bright, round face was especially excited that they were all so happy about it. "Last year, I saw them first," he said, and the family quietly smiled.

"I saw them the very first time," he continued, "but they wouldn't believe me. I kept pointing, but they wouldn't believe me!" He looked exasperated as he remembered the past, but then he grinned happily, "But now they do. They believe me now." Then he looked me in the eye for emphasis, "And they should!"

I love that young man! Yes, we need extra Confirmations to help us break through the times of our own resistance.

He would've liked my real story about the hawk. This is a new hawk story - one I haven't told you yet . . .

One day I was passing through my kitchen/dining room area (wow, exactly where I am writing now!), and I felt a very strong sense that I should look out my bay windows at the tallest fir tree in the greenspace outside my backyard. I tried to fight the feeling - I mean, it wasn't very logical - but I went closer to the windows in order to resolve my feeling.

To my heart's surprise, there was a hawk in the tallest fir tree! It took me aback. After all, this had only been a feeling, a notion that I was placating by actually taking a look. The sturdy hawk sat there, quite at home near some of the top branches. I kept looking at it in amazement, then glancing away, and then looking back - and it was still there!

"This is quite an event. It is so beautiful," I thought. Tears of gratitude came into my eyes. And then I thought of my camera. "Oh heck, by the time I get it, the beautiful hawk nestled in near the topmost branches will be gone."

But I took a breath, and felt compelled to run and get my trusty camera anyway. When I returned, I was shocked all over again - shocked in a good way. For there, amongst the home of the fir tree's branches, sat the hawk, as if settled in. As I clicked the shutter, the hawk sat there, clear as day, as if allowing the photo to be taken for all kinds of purposes.

The only thing that made it the least bit unclear was my hand, as it was shaking all the while.

Just last week, I repeated this story to my friend and CPA, Paul. What I didn't tell Paul as we spoke and worked on my taxes, is that as I looked out the big picture window at the tall fir trees behind him, I saw a large, beautiful hawk perched at the very top of the highest fir tree! Really, it would take me all day to keep repeating all these sacred sightings. And to think, at the beginning of all this, I really didn't see the beautiful, inspiring hawks that Allen had seen so easily.

Today, as I drove through town, another hawk flew over me, this time gliding high overhead on the air currents, and tipping its wings. I accepted Allen's love and sent my love back to him, and drove on *happily along the road* (as one of my last dreams had described).

Now, as I send the many messages of Love and Light from The Mystery School of Grief to you, I'm looking at something I've saved. A special person gave me a short poem, stemming from hearing my stories and also in answer to my assignment for each person in my class to write a Haiku. She put it on a beautiful, purposefully time-worn gift card - with a string hanging loose from it. It simply says:

Red tail hawk
Suspended in time
On currents of heart songs. - Frances Newham

Thank you, Fran. It's still with me.

Many things are still with me. Just last week, I found myself telling my close friend, Sally, about yet another of my many dragonfly visitations, which I'll share here. Sally had also read my story about the Iridescent Blue Dragonfly that visited Jim and myself at our front door the morning after Allen's passing over. She brought something to my attention after looking up dragonflies in "The National Audubon Society's Field Guide to the Pacific NW," by Peter Alden and Dennis Paulson. Her thoughts and discoveries became part of one of my recent columns:

According to Audubon and Sally, the dragonfly is 300 million years old. "It's like it's been here from the beginning," Sally said. It made me smile in the way it dove-tailed with how the dragonfly had been here from the beginning of so much - including from the beginning of my walk with grief.

Over the years, I've had so many visits from dragonflies that I stopped counting. These remarkable visits often come when I am in need of some kind of comfort, but one of the most beautiful times came late one summer. My son, Jim, and I were walking along the shore of Cannon Beach, only to look up and realize we were in a cloud of dragonflies. Not one or two, but an entire, light cloud of them. We'd never seen so many in our life! Then as we walked and talked, we'd look up again, amazed to find they were still there with us, following our path - being a bridge from grieving, into grace, for us.

The Dragonfly Cloud at the beach was beautiful - diaphanous. Jim and I still talk about it. In some ways, I still feel I'm in that diaphanous Cloud of Magic everywhere. The dragonflies were very important to us, but I also feel the importance of the luminous wings of a friend like Sally. Part of our Double Rainbows are the people who share in our path and become real "Earth angels" to us. Then, as each of us shares, one with the other, we give that luminous strength to each other, plus we also get to honor and celebrate the people we love, both on this side and the Other Side of the Veil.

These loving people and loving messages come to us in a wide variety of ways. And at different times. Sometimes the message awaits the perfect moment to reveal itself. As I looked through my assortment of greeting cards, wanting to find the right card for Jim's birthday, I came across a card I purchased on a trip on the Sternwheeler, through the Columbia River Gorge. I bought this greeting card, not to give away, but to save for myself. It is a gorgeous rendition of a hawk, done in a kind of Native American art style.

Even now, I still couldn't bare to part with it, so I put it out on my kitchen island counter - my "mini art gallery." I also put my book notes out on the same counter. One day I turned the card over. This is part of what it said (by Sue Coccia, Earth Art International): *"Hawks . . . help to maintain nature's balance. Their eyesight is the best in the entire animal world. Look inside and see the mountains touching the heavens, the Dragonfly and mystical creatures of the sky. Also in flight find the Ladybug, bringing you happiness and good fortune."*

I really had to smile - and giggle! - all over again. Here, unified all together in one card, were the major symbols of expression from people I love on the Other Side, including Dee now, with her delightful Ladybug!

I hope you think about all these things as you continue on your important path of being a gentle Avatar of Love. I take a deep breath of gratitude as I think about how my boys - my men- have developed their own luminous strength. Just this year, Julian chose a present to give me from both him and Jim. He had chosen a beautiful, light green dragonfly, and I've worn it throughout the writing of this book. In the course of these years of healing, Julian's heart has grown big with love and compassion. We are all close. And Jim has leaned into it, and shared the path of seeing so much more than what's on the surface of things.

"Poem for My Boys"

Each time I see a good man
or a true Hero in a movie -
I think of Dad (Allen).
I still do.

Only now, when I see
a good man or a kind Hero,
I think of each of you.
I see Dad in you - so clearly.

I am so proud of my boys - my men.

Allen, too, still has his ways of being a Hero to me. One day, when it was long overdue, I cleaned out one of his bureau drawers. In it I found a carefully taken care of collection of Love Notes. These were the Love Notes I'd given to him in the course of our busy days. They were little notes. Maybe some men would not have saved them. They were of little things - hope you have a good day, honey - etc. Finding the Love Notes I'd written to him, to help us stay in touch during our work days, made my heart enormously happy. Sometimes you don't know how much the little things you do mean to someone you love.

I am so glad we have kept on sharing.

In the same way, I include this next poem, as a way of continuing to share in this ephemeral fashion, with him now. It is an Act of Sacred Devotion. I wrote it during the Hawaiian vacation with the boys, and I paired the poems with a photo of a line of Palm Trees beside the ocean. In my print, the words are placed between the Palm Trees. Together, they become a new vision of togetherness. (I hope to make this available as a print, so you may obtain it and frame it for hanging in your home if you desire. Any additional offerings of prints, stories, poems, etc., will be listed on the website, FlowersOfTheSpirit.com.) I hope you think of your Loved One as you read this:

"Like Palm Trees to the Sky"

There is a place
where two worlds meet
where both pain and hope
sit side by side.
For you are there,
in death,
and I am here,
in life.
Two worlds apart,
supposedly.
But as I stand in just this place
I see that palm trees do not live alone,
and Island breezes,
though not visible,
still exist, calling branches
into dance-like partnership.
And so I've come to understand
that I am also there, with you,
on the Other Side,
And you are likewise here
with me, in life.
In this place
where two worlds meet
and dance anew,
hearts knowing I am part of you,
hearts happy you are part of me -
Like Palm Trees
  in the Sky.

Jim helped by using an art mode to make the photo look a bit like a painting. It gives it a magical look. I am glad I wrote this book, just to appreciate, even more fully, all the ways Jim has helped me.

"The Big Place"

Over the lunch table,
my son, Jim, grins at me.
Sunshine pours forth
from a place so sacred
it cannot be contained.
His eyes shine,
knowing where it comes from.
Together we celebrate
the big place.

As I thought about this last chapter, "Double Rainbows" - and all the people who are a part of them, my doorbell rang. I didn't want to be interrupted, but I was glad I answered the door, as it was - interestingly enough - my Schwan's delivery man, Paul. I had been thinking of him, and I took the time to tell him how much we all appreciated his bright and genuinely loving attitude, "coincidentally," so much like Allen's. I said, "You really deserve to know how much your giving attitude means to all of us!"

Then, as he asked me what I was up to, we started discussing Double Rainbows. He clued me in to a good new movie I might like, about similar bountiful, giving attitudes. "But they missed one big thing, in my opinion," Paul added.

"What was that?"

"They missed the secret of giving to another person. Just doing something that makes another person happy."

"Truly," I said, "It makes them happy, and it also makes us so happy to give to someone!"

We both nodded our heads knowingly, enthusiastically.

"And it makes us happy because we are part of each other," I added. "When we give to someone else, we give to the Circle we are a part of. It's like a Rainbow. When we see a Rainbow, we usually only see half of it. But our generous actions connect us, one to the other, and complete the circle we're all a part of. Then we see the whole thing, the entire Rainbow Circle!"

I smiled broadly as I blinked away some good tears. As I was talking, I remembered the first glorious Rainbow that had started us on our path. "Just like the Rainbow Circle my sons and I looked up and saw after Allen's Celebration of Life," I said.

Ahhhhh . . .

And Paul and I shared a big ol' hug.

I talked to Jim on the phone as I started on this final chapter. I told him a few days ago, when I thought I was going to finish this book, that it was again a Full Moon and a full Eclipse, as when Allen passed over, and he so deeply understood. I also see in my journal, these poetic notes about Allen.

"The Light"

so we chat back and forth
moon / sun / moon / sun
and that is love.

On our phone call, Jim is explaining his new video game with me. He talks about his skills with a degree of confidence that I know is well earned, "I've become a good Starship Pilot!"

"I couldn't agree more," I answer, heart to heart, as both of us seek ways to share all the Light - and the Wings - Allen has so lovingly and tenderly given us.

Thank you Allen, and everyone,
for being a part of the Unexpected Miracles
that brighten not only me and my family's lives,
but hopefully the lives of many more.

"The Mystery School of Grief," Secrets:
- Begin with Love -

All grief begins with Love.
Because the Energy of Love is an Eternal Gift,
Love can Grow after our Loss.

#1: Become a gentle Avatar of Love.
> Because grief begins with love, and is based on love, then Love is the foundation, the guiding force of healing.
> If we start there, in love's domain, and let it multiply instead of decrease, our grief will be filled, more and more, with a healing kind of grace - because Love is being activated.

#2: Don't Let Your Loved One Go, Let Your Loved One In.

#3: Love has the Greatest Energy
> In the Energy is the Gifts - to help you Become More, because of Love.

#4: Open your heart; don't close it.
> Grief is a process meant to Open our hearts, not close them.

#5: The Energy of Love (from one heart to another)
> can cross the Barriers of Time and Space

#6: Treasure Moments of Grace

#7: Lift your head & eyes upward, and Ask Questions
> that have the same positive direction.
> What can I Learn & how can I Grow?

#8: Receive a new Lightness of Love from the ways
> your Loved One communicates with you,
> as he or she reflects the Ongoing Love from the Divine.

#9: Joy and Pain can sit side by side.
> Understand the Yin Yang of Opposites,

Use the Wisdom of Balance to create a Healing
Circle within yourself.

#10: Others will help you See into the Miraculous.

#11: Sacred Preparations and Confirmations
         will help you understand the Design of your Life.

#12: Double Confirmations are Double Miracles -
         Spirit sends People and Events
         meant to Awaken your Higher Vision

#13: Let your voice be heard.
         It will clear the skies and mend your Heart -
         by leading you into the Extraordinary.

#14: Speak of your Loved Ones in the Present Tense when you can,
         for they are Alive in spirit.

#15: As you share and listen with others who have suffered,
         it will open up a Circle of Compassion
         that brings more healing to all.

#16: Your Loved Ones will use creative ways to reach you:
         The Radio, TV, Flickering Lights, Dreams, and more!
         Get a Journal, and Write them Down.

#17: Work Lovingly with your Dreams.

#18: Let the healing power of Nature tend you.

#19: Visitation Dreams hold a beauty all their own.
         Let their Love & Inspiration change your Perspective.

#20: Tend Your Heart by Listening to its daily needs.
         Open your heart to your close family & friends,
         so they can tend you, too.

#21: Choose to use Good Energy;
         Decide to Add to the World around you.

#22: Practice Symbolic Actions.
>   Center yourself, by standing in the Circle of Love
>   from your Loved One & Higher Spirit -
>   then find a way to intentionally activate
>   its life-giving power in your daily life.
>   Small symbolic steps have great power.

#23: Use Noticing and Mindfulness.
>   Un-cloud your Mind -
>   to find Wisdom and Guidance.

#24: Be a Bridge of Compassion. Help someone else.

#25: Moments Surrounding Birth & Death
>   Create a Magical Crack between Two Worlds,
>   Allowing a Glimpse into the Mysteries.

#26: Healing Energy has a POWER to it.
>   Let yourself feel it! Ask it to come in.

#27: Tears are Emotionally Healing,
>   but Tears are also Physically Healing.

#28: The Double Blessing: As Spirit flows through us,
>   and our Loved Ones, we all can work in tandem
>   to create a bigger Circle of Healing.

#29: When Dreams of Guidance come,
>   your understanding of them may come later.
>   Track Dreams of Guidance by writing them down.

#30: There is a Centerpoint of Peace and Love.
>   You can find it. It is where everything sacred begins.

#31: Mastery is not perfection.
>   Mastery is the ongoing act of offering up our imperfection,
>   so we might continually BE perfected.

#32: The secret of Mastery is to have a beginner's mind.

#33: Mastery is the Heartfelt Desire, after being Healed,
             to become the Healer, to Give after you have been Given To.

#34: Mastery is to Surrender to the More.

#35: The pain of the Wounded Warrior becomes the Healing Light
             of Compassion that calls a Multitude of Angels into Action.
             Directing our Suffering into Healing is how we get our Wings.

#36: Never Say Your Life is Over; It is Ever a Beautiful, Purposeful
             Work in Progress, so Stay Open to Surprises.

#37: Do not Judge your Ongoing Purposes; Embrace each Relationship
             & Project, and Let your Loved One Help You with it.

#38: If you Notice Mini-Miracles and Creative Messages
             from your Loved One, then they happen More Often.

#39: Be Grateful. Concentrate on Celebrating all the Good Things
             in your Loved One and let that Good continue to Flow into your
             Life.

#40: When you develop gentle Courage, You make an Upward Shift.
             You become an Integral Part of Countless Double Rainbows.

       *- Now you are PART of the beautiful Mysteries you have received.
        And these are the Healing Mysteries your heart will share. -*

In Appreciation

I want to celebrate the love, help, and devotion from these special people. I am ever grateful to Allen - and also to my dear sons, Jim and Julian, who helped me mightily, and became my heroes as they stepped into a beautiful kind of manhood, even during grief. I'm so thankful both of my boys were glad to be part of this book, as they had so much to give. And to John Judy, my sweet surprise, my sunrise - thank you for being my love, and for reading about another love. Your generosity, wisdom and joy have given me new life. Thank you to intuitive and dear friend, Candia Sanders, who helped me on my path through grief, then eventually read the manuscript even while going through one of the hardest times of her life. To Judy Black, my inspiring friend and writing buddy - how could we have done it, if we hadn't written our grief books at the same time? To Sally Lavell, who tended me with her friendship, kindness & laughter so I could write this book with ease. To Aram Levendosky, whose conversations during acupuncture were enlightening. To Bev Martin, who I felt was placed in my life before Allen's passing, in order to be the intuitive angel and friend I needed from the very beginning. And to Kirk Holt, who understood the vast realms of potential in healing from grief and other losses.

I'm also thankful to my departed parents who loved me so much from the Other Side of the Veil that they came in to make amends and start a whole new chapter in our lives. Many other experiences came from the Other Side, including messages from a son of a friend of mine, Del. His son died in a suicide but showed up during Reiki to help his grieving father. It broke through many barriers, created profound healing, and informed this book greatly. Thanks also to my Grief Group for help that will last a lifetime.

I'm also constantly grateful to have a circle of writing friends from my "Writing - for the Life of It!" class at the Sherwood YMCA (through Lauren and Renee's help). Special thanks goes to those who gave their support during the process of writing this book: Fran, Jane, Don, and Dee (departed). Just today, Dee's "ladybug" visited me on my deck. Thank you also to Bill Brennock for ongoing kind support. Appreciation also to my column editor, Ray Pitz, from

"The Sherwood Gazette," who has given me a way to converse on deeper levels. And to Kay Allenbaugh, who opened up new vistas in book writing for me.

All these people are wise, loving, and giving. They helped me during the difficult-to-write parts of this book, and kept me going. Thank you also to all the friends who'd had deep losses, and read the book from the personal vantage point of healing from grief. I think of Carol, Suzanne, Liz, Sheena, Kirk, Sally, Samantha, Candia, Bev, Jack, Judy, Don, Jane and many others who encouraged me to carry on, while saying they enjoyed the book.

And thanks to Tyler Chen, whose computer and design skills, along with his helpful spirit, allowed me to finish the circle, and see "The Mystery School of Grief" come into being - with grace.

When you write a book, it develops your leadership, and it draws people with leadership to you. All these great people have the loving leadership that adds a patina of caring, real-life beauty into this book. I feel this beauty now, as it lifts off and breathes the healing concepts into the air, into the spacious arms of others. Thank you for "lift off." As my son, Jim, said today, "Healing from grief is a group activity."

And last but not least, thank you to Spirit, who walked me through the hard times, when I could not see, and brought me to a place of even greater Light.

Also by author/speaker Sheila Stephens:

Books:
"The Art of Prayer & Tea & Thee;
A New Way to Find a Moment to Pray
in the Midst of Our Busy Days"

Editor of her late husband's book:
"Gone to Glory" (The New Western series)
by Allen Stephens

Newspaper Columns:
"Writing - for the Life of It!", The Sherwood Gazette
"Adventures in Writing 101", The Mountain Times

Sheila Stephens also appears in:
  The "Chocolate for a Woman's Soul" book series
  by Kay Allenbaugh:
    "Chocolate for a Woman's Soul, Vol. II"
    "Chocolate for a Woman's Blessings"
    "Chocolate for a Woman's Courage"
    "Chocolate for a Woman's Dreams"
    "Chocolate for a Teen's Soul"
    "Chocolate for a Teen's Spirit"
    "Chocolate for a Lover's Heart"
  The Oregon Writers Colony,
  "Seasoned with Words"

*More about the author and current availability of newsletters,
other stories, poems & prints at* <u>FlowersoftheSpirit.com</u>

*"Bloomin' stuff! -
Insights to Help Us Grow"*

Made in the USA
San Bernardino, CA
01 October 2015